The growing divide

A social audit
1979–1987

Edited by
Alan Walker and Carol Walker

Child Poverty Action Group
1-5 Bath Street, London EC1V 9PY
June 1987

CPAG, 35.912 (3) [4.95 . 10 87]

Cover drawing by Ingram Pimm
Cover design by Hilary Arnott
Typeset by Boldface Typesetters, London EC1
Printed by Calvert's North Star Press, 31-39 Redchurch Street, London E2

Contents

Abbreviations

CP community programme
EEC European Economic Community
FES Family Expenditure Survey
FIS family income supplement
HB housing benefit
HEC Health Education Council
IMF International Monetary Fund
IS income support
JTS job training scheme
MMA married man's tax allowance
MSC Manpower Services Commission
NEC National Executive Committee
    (of the Labour Party)
NCIP non-contributory invalidity
    pension

NIC national insurance contributions
OPCS Office of Population Censuses
    and Surveys
PSI Policy Studies Institute
RPI retail price index
RSG rate support grant
SB supplementary benefit
SBC Supplementary Benefits
    Commission
SSAC Social Security Advisory
    Committee
SSP statutory sick pay
TOPS training opportunities scheme
UB unemployment benefit
YTS youth training scheme

Contents

Abbreviations

CP community programme
EEC European Economic Community
FES Family Expenditure Survey
FIS family income supplement
HB housing benefit
HEC Health Education Council
IMF International Monetary Fund
IS income support
JTS job training scheme
MMA married man's tax allowance
MSC Manpower Services Commission
NEC National Executive Committee
 (of the Labour Party)
NCIP non-contributory invalidity
 pension

NIC national insurance contributions
OPCS Office of Population Censuses
 and Surveys
PSI Policy Studies Institute
RPI retail price index
RSG rate support grant
SB supplementary benefit
SBC Supplementary Benefits
 Commission
SSAC Social Security Advisory
 Committee
SSP statutory sick pay
TOPS training opportunities scheme
UB unemployment benefit
YTS youth training scheme

Preface

This pamphlet was produced with very little notice and at great speed. Yet again CPAG's staff and friends responded magnificently to calls for assistance. All of the contributors produced their chapters promptly within an extremely tight schedule. Peter Golding, Ruth Lister and Paul Wilding read and commented helpfully on the manuscript and, as well as contributing herself, Hilary Arnott prepared the pamphlet for publication. We owe a debt to David Bull and Paul Wilding, the editors of CPAG's 1983 pamphlet, *Thatcherism and the Poor*, for providing such a clear and authoritative reference point for this volume. We are extremely grateful to all of those who contributed in different ways to the production of this pamphlet.

Alan Walker   April 1987
Carol Walker

About the contributors

Hilary Arnott is Publications Officer with the Child Poverty Action Group

Fran Bennett is Deputy Director of the Child Poverty Action Group

Dominic Byrne is Research Officer with the Low Pay Unit

Huw Edwards is Lecturer in Social Policy and Administration, Manchester Polytechnic

Peter Esam is Head of the Welfare Rights Unit in the London Borough of Greenwich

Caroline Glendinning is a Research Fellow in the Social Policy Research Unit at the University of York

John Hills is Senior Research Fellow in the Suntory Toyota International Centre for Economics and Related Disciplines at the London School of Economics and Political Science

Ruth Lister is Director of the Child Poverty Action Group

Martin Loney is Senior Lecturer in Social Policy, Open University

David Piachaud is Reader in Social Administration, London School of Economics and Political Science

David Taylor is Director of Statistical Research, Unemployment Unit

Peter Townsend is Professor of Social Policy, University of Bristol, and Chairperson of the Child Poverty Action Group

Alan Walker, Professor of Social Policy, University of Sheffield, was formerly a longstanding member of CPAG's Executive

Carol Walker is Senior Lecturer in Social Policy and Administration, Manchester Polytechnic

Steve Winyard is Lecturer in Social Policy, University of Leeds

CHAPTER 1

Introduction: a policy for two nations

Alan Walker

In 1983 CPAG produced a pre-election pamphlet, *Thatcherism and the poor*, which examined the government's record between 1979 and 1983.[1] That pamphlet provides a devastating indictment of the first Thatcher government's indifference and, in some instances, outright antagonism towards poor families and the social services on which they depend. But despite its bad record with regard to the poor, the government was re-elected in 1983 and, therefore, that pamphlet must now be seen as an interim, or perhaps half-term, report on the government's social policies. Now that another election looms, it is the duty of CPAG, as well as something of a tradition – whichever party is seeking re-election – to examine the government's record in respect of the poor. Similar assessments were carried out on the 1964-70 and 1974-79 Labour governments.[2]

The poverty of Thatcherism

The 1983 Conservative manifesto did not mention poverty. Its predecessor, in 1979, mentioned 'poor people' and 'poverty' once each. The appeal to the electorate in 1983 was much the same as in 1979: the defence of freedom, strengthening the rule of law, a sound economy based on free enterprise and individual and family responsibility. There was recognition of the potential damage that unemployment might inflict, but, as David Taylor shows in chapter 8, the response has been continued reliance on the assumed job generation potential of free enterprise, coupled with attempts to define away the problem, rather than with genuine job creation or providing adequate benefits for the unemployed.

As in 1979 there were no explicit policies in the 1983 manifesto for combating poverty. This was, on the face of it, surprising in 1979, since poverty had risen under Labour and this might have been regarded as an Achilles heel. The complete absence of references to poverty or an anti-poverty strategy in 1983 is perhaps less surprising given the huge increase (by nearly 50 per cent) in the numbers living on, below or close to the supplementary benefit (SB) poverty line between 1979 and 1983, described in full in chapter 3.[3] The manifesto did have quite a lot to say about the importance of supporting family life, but the implications for family life of the growing

1

poverty among families with children since 1979 was obviously not regarded as having any bearing on this commitment.[4]

But that was 1983. Now, as the public opinion polls show consistently, the government has an 'uncaring' public image, and when the next manifesto comes we might expect more references to 'protecting the weak and vulnerable'. But will they be convincing? The electorate must be the final judge. Certainly, on the evidence presented in this pamphlet the government will be hard pressed to substantiate a claim to care for or about the poor. The verdict of informed social policy commentators has already been given: the government 'does not feel guilty about the poor' and it is not burdened by a 'social conscience'.[5]

A policy for two nations

We should not be surprised by an apparent lack of concern for the poor or the absence of an explicit anti-poverty strategy. The economic and social strategy on which the government has been embarked since 1979 depends, to a considerable extent, on the promotion of poverty (see chapters 2, 4 and 14). As Martin Loney points out in his consideration of the main elements of the government's strategy, the foundations of Thatcherism are built on the assumption that economic (and, therefore, social) progress will be achieved only if the gap between the two nations of rich and poor is widened.

The first public statement of this central tenet of Mrs Thatcher's personal philosophy can be traced back to a speech she gave to the Conservative Party's annual conference at Blackpool in 1968. She expressed scepticism about the welfare state and its tendency to undermine 'desirable' social values such as self-discipline, hard work and personal responsibility.[6] People should not, she argued, expect the government to solve their problems. This speech marked the beginnings of the departure of the, soon to be reborn, traditional Tories from the, soon to be denigrated, Butskellite path of the one nation Tories. The latter's ambivalence towards capitalism – most famously expressed in Edward Heath's denunciation of its 'unacceptable face' – was replaced through Mrs Thatcher by a passionate belief in free enterprise; a belief that had been locked away in the Tory attic after the war because of its association with the inter-war unemployment and poverty. Of course, the intellectual roots of Thatcherism's belief in discipline, free enterprise and strong central government stretch back much further, via Hayek and Victorian morality, to Adam Smith.

Although, within this 'two nation' philosophy, society is regarded as having a duty to provide minimum standards of income as protection against severe deprivation,[7] there are two reasons why this should not be regarded as a significant commitment. First, despite the lead in the opposite direction provided by Adam Smith's recognition of the social definition of need, poverty is usually defined in restricted, absolute terms rather than by reference to general living standards (see chapters 14 and 15). So, for example, in

2

reviewing the social security system the Department of Health and Social Security (DHSS) attempted to rubbish the long history of authoritative official and independent research on poverty, which points to the need for a relative definition, in favour of a more restricted concern only with those 'in genuine need' or 'whose needs are greatest'.[8]

Second, it is assumed that unfettered free enterprise will automatically result in the abolition of poverty as the incomes of the poorest are pulled up by economic growth and rising standards of living. There is, therefore, no need for an anti-poverty strategy because free enterprise will solve the already minimised problem, with growth, rather than redistribution, as the engine of improvement. This approach was spelt out recently by the paymaster-general in the House of Commons debate on social divisions in British society:

> The government are committed to helping all our citizens share in improved prospects, both in personal incomes and in public services. This can be achieved only through the ability of our economy to create wealth. It is economic growth which can enable us to enjoy higher personal incomes which can both bear the weight of more spending on public services and give us greater personal disposable income.[9]

Unfortunately, as the evidence in chapters 3 and 4 shows unequivocally, the poor have got steadily poorer relative to the rest of the community over the last eight years, despite the much vaunted seven successive years of economic growth. Worse still:

- According to the official Family Expenditure Survey, those in the bottom tenth saw their real incomes drop by 9.7 per cent on average between 1979 and 1985.
- The fall for families with children in the bottom tenth was even greater–between 15.7 per cent and 27.2 per cent according to the number of children.

Contrary to the propaganda, the higher 'telephone figure' incomes of the new entrepreneurs have been derived, in part, from the lower incomes of the poor:

- The top fifth of wage earners have seen their real salaries increase by 22 per cent since 1979–six times the increase in the wages of the bottom fifth.
- In 1986 alone the number of low paid workers increased by 400,000.[10]

As Dominic Byrne shows, the government has pursued a dual wage strategy. On the one hand, high salaries linked to profits have been encouraged and taxes have been cut to enhance them, while, on the other hand, low wages have been stimulated–by privatisation, the abolition of wages council controls and by cutting some social security benefits–as a means of increasing profitability. Rather than sharing in prosperity, increased riches for some have been at the expense of the pauperisation of others.

3

Being economical with the truth
Faced with the potentially uncomfortable contradiction between the rhetoric of free enterprise and the reality of the divisive, self-interested pursuit of individual wealth and the political risk associated with its 'uncaring' face, the government has evolved a, now characteristic, response. When confronted with a problem that cannot be ignored, yet equally cannot be tackled within its rigidly predetermined policy framework, it turns its energies, and those of the civil service, to defining it out of existence. Examples of this disdain for the truth are scattered throughout the pamphlet.

Of course, all governments manipulate the presentation of statistics to suit their own interests, but the Thatcher government has elevated obscurantism to a central role in policy making. In retrospect, it is not surprising to find, in her 1986 speech to the Conservative Party conference, Mrs Thatcher expressing scepticism about the British system of higher education, the main achievement of which seemed to her to be to teach people to criticise and question everything.[11] Nor is it surprising that the first and last years of the 1979-87 Thatcher administrations were marked by controversy about inequalities in health. However, as Peter Townsend shows in chapter 9, the controversy did not surround the *findings* of the Black Committee and Health Education Council, but the attempts to suppress their reports. While thousands of people are literally dying unnecessarily, the government is concentrating on trying to prevent us from getting a clear view of the iceberg the Titanic is heading for.

There are plenty of other examples of a consistent policy of obfuscation in order to cover up social reality and stifle public debate. There was the decision to cancel the annual release of poverty statistics in favour of a bi-annual count and the failure to publish the latest set promptly; the cancellation of the annual monitoring of local social service provision; the restriction of access to official OPCS data on the relationships between health and social class; the suppression of information about the deteriorating condition of the housing stock, and, by the use of various procedural manoeuvres, the avoidance of the statutory necessity to consult the Social Security Advisory Committee about changes in benefit regulations affecting millions of people (see chapter 11).

Perhaps most infamously, the government has carried out 19 changes in the calculation and presentation of the unemployment count since 1979 (the main changes are summarised in chapter 8). The aggregate effect of these changes has been to reduce the 'headline' total by around 500,000. Moreover, ministers were reported recently to be working on a scheme to abandon altogether the monthly unemployment count if the government wins the next election,[12] although this has been denied.

As well as attempting to cover-up the full impact of policies, there has been a growing tendency to 'shoot the messenger' if anyone has dared to question the government's version of reality. The traducement of leading

4

members of the Church of England following the *Faith in the city* report, the attack on leading academics for 'descending into politics' following their criticism of the government's manipulation of the unemployment statistics, and the attempts to smear the facts and arguments advanced by groups such as the Low Pay Unit, the Unemployment Unit, CPAG and others attempting to speak on behalf of the poorest and most deprived victims of present policies, are clear signposts to the nature of the establishment's response to criticism.[13]

Time after time over the last eight years the government has chosen to restrict the public's access to the truth about the social condition of Britain. This emphasises the case made below for an independent social audit of government policies and particularly one that is mindful of the position of the most deprived and vulnerable in our society.

Theme and plan of the pamphlet

Rather than choosing simply to update the service-by-service contributions to the 1983 pamphlet – which would have been repetitive and subject to constant references to 'more of the same' – we have concentrated on the major theme that has asserted itself in the second period of Mrs Thatcher's premiership: the increasingly divided nature of British society, particularly the fissure between rich and poor that has widened into a chasm since 1979. Despite attempts to suppress or shrug them off, a long series of both official and independent reports by a diverse range of authorities – from the OPCS *Social trends* to Lord Scarman, from the Church of England to the Health Education Council – have confirmed what CPAG's own research and contacts with poor families had shown consistently to be the case: that Britain is widely felt to be a more sharply divided society than it was eight years ago.

The authors of this volume assess the evidence behind this commonly held view. They look back to 1979 and not just to the start of the second Thatcher administration. To be fair to the government, it has frequently claimed that its policies were not designed to succeed within only one term of office and we give it the benefit of any doubt by appraising its record over the past eight years. It must be remembered too that the Conservatives did not inherit a very respectable legacy from the previous Labour government: poverty and unemployment had increased; public expenditure cuts had been carried out, especially on capital spending, and the nil-cost review of the SB scheme had attracted widespread opposition.

Like the editors of the previous CPAG volume we were faced with a dilemma concerning what had been labelled 'Thatcherism'. Although the basic elements of this approach have long been present in the neo-liberal wing of the Conservative Party and, therefore, in Peter Golding's words, the epithet is an 'absurd flattery of its heroine',[14] there is no doubt that the policies of the 1979-87 Conservative governments have been abnormally closely associated with the personal philosophy of its leader. Thus, despite

5

reasonable academic reservations about the aura of coherence and consistency that this lends to current Conservative policies – witness the reported 'death' of monetarism in October 1986[15] – we have decided to follow our immediate predecessors, as well as the current convention among informed commentators, and refer to the characteristic approach of the Conservative government as 'Thatcherism'.

A final point about the terms of reference the editors provided for the authors and the sub-title of this pamphlet requires elaboration. Although economic policy has tended to dominate social policy under both Labour and Conservative governments, the period 1979-87 has seen the complete subordination of the latter to the former, to an extent unprecedented in the post-war period.[16] Reflecting its neo-monetarist philosophy, the government has been peculiarly concerned with a very narrow economic perspective on key issues affecting British society – inflation, public expenditure, employment, taxation, health and so on – and the social and human dimensions of these issues have received even less attention than hitherto. This approach was characterised by CPAG, in 1979, as 'Abandoning social priorities'.[17] The increasing domination of this approach over the last eight years – together with the assertion, based on conviction rather than reasoned argument, that 'There is no alternative' – has stultified public debate about the social condition of Britain, the social consequences of government policy and the need for alternative policies.

The authors of this volume believe that responsible and balanced policies, which serve the interests of the whole population, cannot be constructed on the basis of the narrow concern with economic efficiency that has dominated the Thatcher government. The pamphlet is an attempt, therefore, to begin to redress this gross imbalance, by stressing the need for a social audit of all policies to put alongside the economic one. Thus, whenever policies are judged, on the face of it, to be a good thing in economic terms, policy-makers and commentators should also ask about their social impact.

The detailed information provided in this pamphlet should serve to remind policy-makers that all, apparently value neutral and scientific, economic policies have social consequences and that a consideration of these consequences must, once again, be given priority. Our concern is with the foreseen, as well as the incidental, impact on the poor. It used to be a truism that the yardstick by which to measure a civilised society is the way it treats its weakest and most vulnerable members. *By the weight of evidence and argument presented here, Britain in the mid-1980s is rapidly losing its claim to be a civilised society.*

The pamphlet is divided into three sections. The first considers the social strategy pursued by the Conservative government since 1979 and the resulting rapid growth in poverty and inequality.

The second group of chapters looks at the specific social costs of the government's policies and the way they have been borne disproportionately

6

by the poor. Two particular groups are singled out for consideration: poor women and poor black people, on the grounds that the government's policies have impinged especially harshly on them. Thus, as Caroline Glendinning shows, one of the major accomplishments of Britain's first woman prime minister has been to preside over the impoverishment of women on a huge scale.

Moreoever, women, black people and other poor groups are often marginalised in official pronouncements about the economic needs of the country. Thus, the impression is given that they are not relevant to the serious business of enterprise, on which Britain's future is said to be based, and as a consequence they will not be entitled to full citizenship in the new economic order that the government is trying to create. We also consider the impact of the government's policies on two crucial determinants of poverty and deprivation: unemployment and health. But, as befits a CPAG publication, greatest weight in this section is given to social security.

We conclude our social audit by looking at the main themes in the stategy to which British society has been subjected over the last eight years. We assess the significance of Conservative policies and draw together the main conclusions about their social consequences. The second part of the conclusion shows that, contrary to the propaganda of the Tory government, there is a responsible and viable alternative. Furthermore, there *is* plenty of evidence that the majority of the British public believe that there is an alternative to the politics of selfishness.

Government attempts to re-write history in terms of the importance of Victorian values have not, as Ruth Lister points out, succeeded in obscuring the equally important collectivist and altruistic values in the British political tradition. Uncomfortably for the government, despite the constant barrage of exhortations for self-reliance and self-interest, these collective impulses keep reasserting themselves in the public opinion polls. These provide the basis for our case against the current strategy and our hope that an alternative approach will be adopted by whatever Party is elected. Economic 'success' built on the foundations of grotesque inequalities, pauperisation and the illness and premature death of the poor in fact spells, as the contributors to this pamphlet show, economic and social disaster.

CHAPTER 2

A war on poverty or on the poor?

Martin Loney

'If you believe economic salvation can only be achieved by rewarding success and the national income is not increasing, then you have no alternative but to make the unsuccessful poorer.'

Reg Prentice, Minister for Social Security, 1979

It is individual families–children, women and men–that must live daily with the burdens and bear the scars of the poverty, deprivation and social divisions created and exacerbated by the Conservative government. But the most lasting impact of Thatcherism will probably be ideological– particularly concerning the role of the state. Gradually, over the last eight years, the government has created, in some circles at least, what Peter Golding has called a new 'common sense' about social policy.[1]

The full significance of the government's ideological impact–in helping to legitimate, in some quarters, the most divisive series of policies introduced since the war–has only recently become clear. We do not want to overstate the extent of the government's influence on attitudes because, as Alan Walker and Ruth Lister point out in their conclusions, there is plenty of evidence of the continuance of a strong altruistic and collectivist spirit in Britain–despite eight years of Conservative government, working in tandem with a largely supportive popular press. However, it is the creation of a new conventional wisdom in official and media circles that both explains the apparent ease with which the government can reduce the incomes of the poorest and makes it so difficult to propose alternative policies.

The main thrust of government policy has been on the economic front. As Alan Walker has pointed out in chapter 1, this economic strategy is based on clear social assumptions–particularly which groups in society should prosper and which should decline–and not surprisingly, therefore, it has had overt, and in some cases severe, social consequences.[2] Economic considerations have also dominated social policy-making–one of the reasons why the government has been able to pursue a concerted attack on the rights of poor families to benefits and services. Appeals to economic probity, financial prudence and sound currency have served to deflect potential criticism– even though, as we see in chapter 4, it is a matter of prudence towards the poor and profligacy towards the rich.

8

There are two further reasons why Thatcherism has been particularly potent in the field of social policy. First, in the pursuit of several key policies it has been able to play to its undoubted strength of populist ideology: self-help, family responsibility and anti-bureaucracy. Second, it has been able to reduce statutory support for some of the poorest and most deprived at little political cost, either because its own natural supporters are not hurt or because it still leaves a majority of winners against the increasingly impoverished set of losers. It is not only the rich who have got richer in recent years; the 'average' worker is also better off. The wageless and the low paid have fallen further and further behind what David Shepherd, Bishop of Liverpool, has called 'comfortable Britain'.

The purpose of this chapter is to take the assessment of Thatcherism as social policy on from *Thatcherism and the poor*. In that pamphlet Peter Golding outlined the essential ingredients of the Thatcher government's approach: privatisation, reviving the informal sector, domestication, selectivity, marketing welfare, social control and obfuscation.[3] While all of these elements are still present, many of the assumptions underlying them and their relative significance in the overall package have become clearer since 1983. This is demonstrated by focussing on the three main aspects of government policy which impinge on the poor: the inequality strategy, the attack on public services and policies towards the family.

The strategy of inequality

The growth of inequality and poverty under the Thatcher governments is not an accidental offshoot from some broader social and economic vision or part of a general short-term sacrifice to ensure long-term economic success. Rather, it is the intended and inevitable outcome of the government's policies. In fact, the immiseration of a growing section of the population may be seen as an episode in the longstanding struggle to maintain the status and privileges of the rich. In that sense, as the formidable Keynesian economist Joan Robinson observed, monetarism has been no more than a convenient fig leaf to legitimate the war against the poor.

American new rightist George Gilder has offered the apt aphorism: 'What the poor need most of all in order to succeed is the spur of their poverty.'[4] Incentives are necessary not only in the form of benefit cuts to the poor, to encourage them to seek work, but also in tax cuts to the rich, to encourage them to work harder (see chapter 4). The very nature of a capitalistic economy, it is argued, puts a premium on the role of the entrepreneur and legitimates the high rewards they receive. Entrepreneurs must be allowed to retain wealth for the practical reason that only they, collectively, can possibly know where it should go, to whom it should be given.[5]

British right-wing authorities, backed by well-funded think tanks–like the Institute of Economic Affairs, the Social Affairs Unit, the Centre for

Policy Studies and the Adam Smith Institute–have been equally enthusiastic in their assaults on welfare measures. For example, on the question of poverty they have generally joined with the views of Sir Keith Joseph, who argued in 1979: 'By any absolute standard there is very little poverty in Britain today.'[6] Benefit levels have been attacked for being too generous and destroying work incentives. Poverty researchers are denounced for exaggerating the numbers of those in poverty and deflecting attention away from the needs of the 'real' poor (a group who, conveniently, remain undefined).[7]

In the topsy turvey world of the new right ideologue poverty is the creation of the naive if well-meaning reformer, who through a plethora of income support programmes and an army of social workers destroys the incentive for self-sufficiency and creates a multitude of welfare recipients reared on a diet of dependency.

Similarly, with state intervention in the labour market, far from assisting the under-privileged, it simply entrenches them further in dependency. Thus David Marsland, deputy director of the Social Affairs Unit, argues:

> In the labour market as much as in any other sphere, dogmatic egalitarianism reduces opportunities and causes inequities. A free market undistorted by state wage controls would enable the young, blacks and women to price themselves back into employment and afford them the opportunity to compete for better jobs and a better life.[8]

From this perspective the abolition of the wages councils, the elimination of the Fair Wages Resolution, the privatisation of ancillary services, the weakening of the trade unions, the reduced role for the factory inspectorate are no more than steps on the road to the liberation of the poor. Once freed from state fetters the market, it is asserted, will allow individuals equal opportunities to employment and earnings. This denial of fact and experience accumulated over the last 100 years, which points to the discriminatory operation of the free market, is another important element in the government's strategy of inequality. The production of inequalities by unregulated employment and wage systems is regarded as 'fair', for example by Lord Young (see p.135), because these reflect differences in personal attributes and skills.

Up with the rich

> 'What is it that impels the powerful and vocal lobby in Britain to press for greater equality . . . Often the reasons boil down to an undistinguished combination of envy and what might be termed "bourgeois guilt".'
>
> *Margaret Thatcher, 1975*

A variety of different factors have been at work in increasing and deepening poverty under the two Thatcher governments (chapter 3). The government's own commitment to widening inequality as one aspect of its broader vision of an enterprise culture has already been noted. This means that tax cuts have been directed disproportionately to the rich, whilst a variety of measures have been used to reduce the value of benefits available to the poor, from the ending of the link between pensions and other long-term benefits and average earnings to the removal of the immediate right of school-leavers to claim benefit. As Dominic Byrne shows in chapter 4, the top 3 per cent of tax-payers have received no less than one-quarter of the total tax cuts.

Simultaneously, the market has also worked to generate widening inequalities, spread further by the government's privatisation programme. Government rhetoric has expiated the guilt of the rich and given them a licence to pursue the politics of greed, secure in the knowledge that in seeking every higher income they were simply securing the incentives required for real effort. In no time at all £50,000 salaries in the City of London could be described as really quite ordinary. In the newly privatised industries directors' salaries soared. Income Data Services reported, in 1987, that it was not uncommon to find top executives on pay of £300,000, some 30 times the average earnings of full-time male manual workers. This might be contrasted with the findings of the Royal Commission on the Distribution of Income and Wealth, in 1975, when top executives had to make do with a salary a mere 18 times that of male manual workers.

Down with the poor

'The rich admire the poor less and less, partly because the poor are not as poor as they used to be, but also because the poor fritter their money on such trash–video cassettes and cars with fluffy mice that joggle in the back window.'
Ferdinand Mount, former adviser to No 10 Downing Street, 1982

If the rich were to find their efforts, or simply their good fortune, ever more lavishly rewarded, albeit in the name of stimulating more general economic benefits, the new philosophy has held out an altogether different prospect for the poor.

Previous governments of all shades have seen the maintenance of full employment as a central role of social and economic policy. What is distinctive about the Thatcher government is its willingness simultaneously to use unemployment as a means of achieving other goals, whether curbing inflation, weakening the trade unions or attempting to force down wage levels, whilst at the same time mounting unprecedented attacks on the victims of these policies.[9]

Thus, the unemployed and other poor families have had the real level of a number of their benefits reduced by such measures as the abolition of the earnings-related supplement, or by the more characteristically low profile chiselling away at the edges, as in the steady cut in the real value of national insurance children's additions (and their total abolition in the case of short-

11

term benefits), or by the savings, in 1985, of £17 million by paying new claimants two weeks in arrears. Further losses are in store for many poor families under the Social Security Act 1986 (see chapters 11-13).

At the same time, as Carol Walker shows in chapter 11, much greater prominence has been given to policing benefit recipients. Indeed, it sometimes seems that the response of government and its supporters to the scale of poverty and unemployment has been to focus public attention on the allegedly excessive 'generosity' of the benefit system, on the one hand, and the 'abuse' of it by the poor, on the other.

While high salaries and the abolition of the top rates of tax are regarded as essential to promote enterprise, the argument that the unemployed are work shy depends for its political success on convincing the public that life on the dole is really not too bad. Thus, in a dramatic front-page story the *Daily Express* announced: 'Better off on the Dole' (23 April 1985) and proceeded, by incorporating a series of unsustainable assumptions, to show that a man with a wife and two children, earning £150 per week, would be only £2.44 better off than on the dole. To achieve this politically important, yet statistically illiterate, conclusion the *Express*-with the assistance of Tory MP Ralph Howell, who placed the question in the House of Commons which 'uncovered' this 'fact'-made some questionable assumptions. It was assumed that in the case of the unemployed, both the husband and wife earned the maximum £4 per week disregarded income, though DHSS figures show that only 1.3 per cent of men and 12 per cent of women, receiving benefit, have part-time earnings. Rent and rate payments were also raised well above DHSS-assumed levels.

Nonetheless, whilst serious researchers point to the awful drabness of life on supplementary benefit,[10] such stories succeed in conveying an entirely different picture. The imposition of a new 'available for work' test-expected to reduce the unemployment register by a further 4 per cent-will constitute an additional barrier for claimants. It is the latest of a long series of measures which attempt to shift the blame for their plight to the innocent victims of the government's own policies. It is clearly irrelevant that many of those driven off the register bear no resemblance whatsoever to Fleet Street's well-known scroungers. In Reading, for example, among those denied benefit, through being judged unavailable for work, was a 59-year-old divorcee with arthritis, looking after a seriously ill mother, who declared herself available for work only a few hours per day, believing she would, at best, receive only part-time work.

The introduction of a pilot scheme in Newton Abbot, Devon, aimed at 'over-50s' sought to enforce an available-for-work test on those claiming unemployment benefit. Two hundred and three claimants in the age group were sent a questionnaire testing their availability for work. Some 90 people subsequently had their benefit suspended, pending review by the adjudication officer. Only the presence of a number of claimants who had been previously involved in an active claimants' association and the support of local political activists and academics prevented the DHSS from driving most of these off the register. In the event, only one claimant was ultimately disqualified.[11] In this case the DHSS clearly failed in its objective, but only after causing immeasurable hardship.

Criminalising the poor

The Right has also done its best to maintain the high profile of the dishonest scrounger. Historians will no doubt find it particularly ironic, though undoubtedly politically convenient, that as real unemployment reached unprecedented levels the media continued to be preoccupied, not with the plight of the growing army of the impoverished, but with the 'scroungers' who were said to be milking the DHSS.

The DHSS has increased the number of social security investigators while the Department of Employment set up its own regional benefit investigation team. The pinnacle of achievement in this regard must be 'Operation Sting'.

In this episode DHSS fraud investigators, aided by members of the Thames Valley Police, rounded up no less than 283 claimants in Oxford in 1983. Charges could only be found against 179 of them. Nonetheless, the police claimed to have uncovered a £15 million fraud and this ensured nationwide headline coverage. Since the operation cost £180,000, this appeared to be good value. However, it was no doubt fortunate for the reputation of the police that the information that resulting prosecutions concerned amounts totalling less than £20,000 was confined to a few lines in the weightier papers.

The single homeless who were the victims, rather than the villains, of this drama received draconian treatment at the hands of the Oxford magistrates, who, in their enthusiasm to set an example, even jailed those who, as it subsequently transpired, had broken no DHSS regulations.[12]

Privatising and marketing welfare

'The welfare state has gradually changed from the expression of compassion to an instrument of political repression unequalled in British history.'
Harris and Seldon, Institute of Economic Affairs, 1979

From the viewpoint of progressive social reformers post-war governments have frequently failed to match their rhetorical concern for the poor or their commitment to equality of opportunity with a political programme which has substantially changed the quality of life for the disadvantaged. Such charges cannot be made against the Thatcher government. Indeed, this government's problem is rather the reverse, for the challenge here is to find politically viable and electorally acceptable ways of diminishing publicly provided health and social services and reducing the redistributing impact of the tax system.

Privatising cleaning

The poor are to be priced into work by benefit cuts, on the one hand, and wage cuts, on the other. Government rhetoric often portrays its role as the defence of the weak against the strong, but in practice it has often been the spearhead of the attacking forces. Thus, for example, in the privatisation of office-cleaning the government drives forward the contracting-out process, abolishes the Fair Wages Resolution which might have provided residual protection for the wages of those affected, and then takes the lead in negotiating new, lower price contracts on the basis of the reduced wage levels that the industry now pays. Simultaneously, the government pursues policies in the economic sphere which guarantee a rising tide of candidates eager for employment at any level of pay, and, in the benefits field, seeks to restrict entitlement and benefit levels in order to ensure that even the lowest wages will still be preferable to state benefits.

The abandonment of the government's role as protector of the lowest paid for one which has meant their further impoverishment is a measure of the change which the Thatcher administration has brought about in the perception of the role of government.

Private medicine: wealth for the rich, hardship for the poor

It is not only in industry or in the City that inequality became more marked. The government's commitment to continuing the wide inequalities in pay within the national health service (NHS) went hand in hand with enhanced opportunities for the medical profession to develop lucrative private practice. Unable to abolish the NHS, the government has had to be content with doing what it can to encourage the growth of the private medical market. NHS consultants are free to make a more active contribution to private medicine, not infrequently at new private hospitals, conveniently located to maximise the parasitic relationship with NHS facilities. As queues for treatment have lengthened, better-off patients could be skilfully manoeuvred from NHS lists to private treatment. For the poor this has afforded little comfort; indeed, it has ensured that some of the sharper elbows of the middle class were removed from the demand for greater NHS resources.

Here, as elsewhere, the operation of the market has produced unequal results. The commitment to the growth of a greater role for the private sector in health care may have ensured greater affluence for the already wealthy consultant, but for the hospital cleaner it has frequently meant lower wages, longer hours and the withdrawal of occupation related benefits.

Second-class treatment for the poor

Not only have claimants been subject to a number of benefit cuts, but, particularly in declining urban areas, they have also been offered an ever less adequate level of services. Housing benefit is a case in point. The govern-

14

ment's eagerness to shift responsibility for the administration of housing benefits to local authorities combined with its unwillingness to provide any further finance, produced what one expert described as 'the largest administrative shambles of the post-war welfare state'.[13] Countless examples emerged of housing benefit not being paid for months.

In DHSS offices the government's commitment to cutting back on the civil service added a further twist. Thus, for example, between 1980 and 1982 it was estimated that the workload in DHSS offices on Merseyside increased by 70 per cent, yet staff levels were still cut back. According to a contemporary report by the Society of Civil and Public Servants, some 100,000 potential claimants in the area were not taking up their supplementary benefit and £17 million in potential benefits was unclaimed. This was not an isolated incident. In the West Midlands, staff cuts and mounting pressure from claimants resulted in a strike in the Birmingham area which lasted from September 1982 to May 1983.

The government's indifference to the plight of the victims of its economic policies was nowhere better illustrated than in its failure to take prompt action to end that dispute, during which claimants received only a flat-rate benefit. Thus, one claimant, who before the strike was receiving £110 per week for his wife and three teenage children, subsequently received only £40 per week in emergency payments.

Today, inner-city DHSS offices – especially in London – continue to operate under severe stress. Claimants often wait all day to be seen. Staff turnover in London is around 50 per cent annually and the error-rate in some offices is over 50 per cent. Research by the Policy Studies Institute has found that nationally six out of seven DHSS staff are under too much pressure to give each task enough attention. Across the country hundreds of thousands of claims remain outstanding for many weeks, in spite of the urgency of the need. According to the Greater London CABx service, the supplementary benefit system is near to breakdown in many London offices.

To have or to have nothing: the rising tide of homelessness

> 'The coroner's jury returned a verdict of accidental death this summer on 14-month-old Debbie Beattie who plunged down several floors in the Mount Pleasant Hotel in London's Kings Cross. Last year an open verdict was recorded on the deaths of Samin Karim and her children Nizemul and Shalha, aged 5 and 4, who died in a hotel fire in Marylebone.'
>
> Roof, *September/October* 1986

We have focussed mainly on the treatment of the poor in the benefit system, but we should not ignore the impact of the government's other efforts to redraw the parameters of British life.

In the housing field the government's antipathy to public sector housing has seen a shift of subsidy away from council tenants towards owner-occupiers. Public sector housing is in decline, with little new building, the most desirable housing sold off at substantial discounts and the housing prospects of the poorer members of society apparently permanently blighted. Today there are no less than 1.5 million on council waiting-lists.

For all the government's commitment to a revitalised private rented market, the inevitable consequence has been the growth in homelessness. Accurate figures are impossible to establish. Last year 100,000 were accepted as priority homeless, though a report by Shelter found growing evidence that many families in bed and breakfast accommodation had never been accepted as homeless by the relevant local authority. For example, a survey in Reading of homeless households in which there were children or a first child was expected, living in bed and breakfast hotels, found that 62 per cent had not been accepted by the council as homeless and therefore did not appear in the official statistics.[14] Nonetheless, we can provide some indicators of the magnitude of the change.

DHSS board and lodging payments for the homeless cost £503 million in 1984, compared with only £52 million in 1979. In London local authorities spent £26 million on bed and breakfast accommodation for homeless families in 1985, a sevenfold increase since 1981.

These stark figures provide little indication of the awful reality of homelessness. For some, as the Shelter report indicated, placement in inadequate bed and breakfast accommodation, far from being a stepping-stone to re-housing, can have fatal consequences. For others, it may permanently blight their family relationships and their children's health and life-chances.

The party of the family

'The family must be the centre of our thinking.'

Sir Keith Joseph, 1975

The Thatcher government has made much of its commitment to the family. One prominent supporter, Paul Johnson, bemoaning the lack of action in this area, recently suggested that the family must be one of the major issues in the next election campaign. The Conservative Family Campaign, backed by a number of MPs and public moralists, is explicit in its commitment to the reconstruction of the archetypical middle-class Victorian family:

The Conservative Family Campaign aims to put the father back at the head of the family table, he should be the breadwinner, he should be responsible for his children's actions. He should be respected by those who teach his children. He should be upheld by social workers, doctors, and others who professionally come into contact with his children. Years of militant feminism, and harmful legislation like the Equal Opportunities Act have undermined the clear biblical concept of the father.[15]

The campaign is the authentic voice of that brand of moral authoritarianism which increasingly seeks to project a selective model of Thatcherism, less focussed on the economic sphere and more concerned with the mobilisation of a wider range of public concerns and fears. For the moral authoritarian there is no equivocation about blaming the victim: crime, poverty, vandalism, inner-city decline are all the outcome of the shiftless attitudes of a people dependent for too long on the nanny state instead of the 'traditional' nuclear family.

In this 'vision', Britain's problems will no longer be solved simply by monetarist economic policies, but only when these go hand in hand with the remoralisation of society.

Market forces and the family

The Achilles' heel of the government's proclaimed commitment to the family is that the reality of Tory policies erodes family life. Lower benefit levels, higher unemployment, increasing inequality and economies in education and social services, rising crime and anti-social behaviour all increase stress, particularly among low income families. At the same time, immigration policies have helped divide many families.

The proposition that the family is a quintessentially Conservative preserve, or a cornerstone of a free enterprise society, is in any case highly suspect. In America, that most admired of free enterprise societies, the divorce rate is rocketing and the family more celebrated in moral mythology than in social reality. The American critic, Christopher Lasch, has noted the link between the wider values of free enterprise America, with its endless search for novelty and its transformation of social life into an odyssey of consumption, and the decline of the family.

> It is the logic of consumerism that undermines the values of loyalty and permanence and promotes a different set of values that is destructive of family life. The need for novelty and fresh stimulation becomes ever more intense, intervening interludes of boredom are increasingly intolerable.[16]

The Thatcher government shares the American obsession with consumerism, whilst denying large numbers of the population anything more than a seat in the stalls from which to watch. A sanctimonious rhetoric about the family goes hand in hand with the erosion of the family as the major social institution. For all the cant and humbug about the family-primarily seen as the provider of care, nurturing and protection to children-the government appears to have shown scant regard for the increasing numbers growing up in deprivation that owes much to its own economic policies.

During the period of the Thatcher government the real level of child benefit has fallen (see chapter 3). There has been mounting concern over child abuse, in part a reflection of the harsh reality of family life for some children. NSPCC figures, issued last year, found that between 1984 and

1985 there was a 68 per cent increase in reports of children seriously or fatally injured and a 42 per cent increase in the number placed on child abuse registers. The poor and the unemployed are particularly vulnerable. Brian Roycroft, Director of Social Services in Newcastle, commented recently that there were an estimated 17,000 children in that city living in 'severe poverty' and a concomitant rapid growth in child neglect and abuse.

Conclusion: the decline in civility

'The truth is, as history has so often shown us, that unfettered market forces lead to the rich and the strong growing richer and stronger and the poor and the weak poorer and weaker until some conflagration in society acted to restore the balance.'

Edward Heath, 1985

There is more to life than simply the economics of daily existence. If we turn away from this area, where the poor have certainly suffered enormous harm, to the wider question of the quality of life, again we find that it is the poorest who have experienced the greatest hardship.

It is the poor who have borne the greatest burden from the increase in crime, up by some 50 per cent since 1979. It is the children of the poor who are most likely when they leave school not only to be unemployed but to remain so. It is the poor who pay the highest price for the deliberate under-funding of municipal services – from the undermining of public transport to the run-down of public parks and leisure facilities.

The rich have their private swimming pools. Their children will always get jobs, if not in the family firm then in that of a friend or through the privileged access to Oxbridge provided by the private school system, and thence into the civil service, the City or one of the well-paid professions. Faced with the public squalor which is an increasingly visible aspect of contemporary urban Britain, the rich can retreat to the leafy suburbs or the newly gentrified and well-protected areas carved out of declining working-class communities. The children of the rich may flirt with drugs, sometimes even fatally, but they are not condemned to be raised in housing estates where drug addiction has become a way of life, where pushers lurk on the stairways and the police drug squad appears, at best, incompetent in the face of a crisis that requires preventive measures rather than reactive policies.[17]

The grotesque inequality of contemporary Britain ultimately demeans us all. The mindless violence; the drug abuse and the related crime; the cynicism of the young, whose futures have been sacrificed on the, now conveniently discarded, altar of monetarism; the sleazy attempt to pin the blame for all of this on the victims of the government's economic policies; the ever more hysterical attempts of Fleet Street to find new scapegoats for

18

our social ills; the elevation of greed into a national religion – all of these are cancers eating away at our country.

In eight years the Thatcher government has not achieved the abolition of the welfare state or the civilised values on which it was founded, but it has had the chance to show us how far, given the opportunity, it can divide Britain.

CHAPTER 3

The growth of poverty

David Piachaud

One century ago in Ireland, while potatoes continued to be exported and there was a surplus of wheat, one million people died of starvation. It was argued by politicians that there was no alternative; markets must be allowed to take their course. Perhaps in one century's time people will look back at the world in the 1980s in the way most people now look back at the Irish potato famine. With the Third World encumbered by debts of one million billion dollars, vast surpluses of food accumulate in some parts of the world. While there is ever more affluence for a fraction of the world's population, millions die of malnutrition and poverty-related diseases.

Similarly, if less starkly, future historians looking back at Britain in the 1980s may examine the economic statistics and point to a period of exceptional and sustained growth in gross national product, rising labour productivity, declining inflation, a broadening base of home- and share-ownership. They may record economic growth, pronounce that it was good and, having writ, move on. Such an historian might be forgiven, for there are many in Britain alive today who content themselves with the colour supplement view of the world in which nothing must be allowed to disturb the cosy complacency of Conservative Britain.

Yet what lies beneath this image? At a political level, there is Conservative rhetoric of helping people to stand on their own feet, encouraging individual opportunity and economic independence from the state—goals that may be shared by many, not only Conservatives. Have these goals been achieved? At a social level, there is an underlying Conservative belief that untrammelled market forces serve the whole community and that all benefit from the pursuit of economic growth. Has this been the case?

The purpose of this chapter is to examine the evidence about the numbers of people in poverty and dependent on social security over the last eight years. The evidence used is entirely official, government surveys and statistics (the sources for all the data are listed in the references at the end of the pamphlet). First, we examine definitions of poverty and levels of benefit. Second, we trace the numbers dependent on social security. Third, those below the poverty level are considered. Finally, we look at evidence about changes in the overall extent of poverty and inequality.

Definitions of poverty and levels of supplementary benefit

In assessing changes in the numbers above and below the poverty line, the first requirement is to be clear and consistent about what is meant by 'poverty'. Here, as in most recent British studies, the supplementary benefit (SB) level will be used to define poverty. This is the level of requirements prescribed by the government and used to determine benefits for those eligible – principally pensioners, disabled and unemployed people, and one-parent families. From April 1987, the weekly levels, excluding housing costs which are added separately, are as follows:

	SB ordinary rate		SB long-term rate
Single person	£30.40		£38.65
Couple	£49.35		£61.85
Child aged 0 - 10		£10.40	
11 - 15		£15.60	

If the SB levels are raised, it is inevitable that more people will fall below the level and more people will be eligible to receive SB; this may be seen as a problem by the government even if it is of benefit to the recipients. But it does mean that changes in numbers on or below SB level may be affected by changes in the level of the benefits. If you move the 'goal-posts', you are likely to alter the score (as has not escaped the government's attention in relation to unemployment statistics – see chapter 8).

The changes in SB levels between 1978 and 1987 are shown in table 1. Overall, in money terms the benefit level has almost doubled from £19.90 to £38.65 per week for a single person on the ordinary rate. Such an increase of itself is, however, meaningless. Over the same period the retail price index (RPI) excluding housing costs rose by 86 per cent; this is perhaps the index that is most appropriate in assessing changes in SB level, since housing costs are added separately in SB calculations. (However, it should be noted that the 'all items' RPI rose by considerably more and estimates of recent price rises as they affect low income households suggest they are higher than the averages cited here). Using the RPI excluding housing costs, there has been a *real* rise in SB level of about 5 per cent since 1978. Thus, the SB poverty level has risen and those on SB in April 1987 are some 5 per cent better off in absolute terms than in November 1978. (As a result of the restructuring of the children's scale rates in 1980, the real value of SB for children of certain ages has increased by more than 5 per cent.) Yet before celebrating this fact it is necessary to consider what has happened to the incomes of others.

Table 1 shows the increase in gross average earnings and in personal disposable income per capita. While the former has risen by 136 per cent since 1978, compared to the increase of some 95 per cent in SB levels, it may be argued that this gross figure does not take into account the increasing burden of taxation (or, more precisely, of national insurance contributions).

21

Table 1: *Changes in SB levels November 1978–April 1987*

Supplementary benefit	
ordinary rate	
single person	+ 95.5%
couple	+ 95.4%
long-term rate	
single person	+ 94.2%
couple	+ 96.0%
Retail price index excluding housing	+ 86%
Retail price index all items	+ 96%
Average gross earnings	+ 136%
Personal disposable income per capita	+ 122.5%

The increase in personal disposable income per capita does provide an indication of overall income levels taking into account all forms of income and deductions for direct taxation; it has risen since 1978 by 122.5 per cent in money terms and 14 per cent in real terms. Thus, compared with incomes in general, SB levels have fallen considerably – for a couple on the ordinary rate from 61 per cent of personal disposable income per capita in 1978 to 53 per cent in 1987.

There have been shorter periods when, as social security ministers have argued, SB levels have kept pace with average incomes, but there have been other spells when they have fallen behind more. The overall picture since the Conservatives took office is of those dependent on SB falling further behind the rest of the population.

Thus, SB levels have maintained and slightly increased their value under the Conservative government, but they have fallen behind the incomes of others and, relatively, the level is lower than in 1978. The answer to the question 'Have the poorest maintained their share of total income?' is 'No'.

Numbers on social security

A commonly stated objective of the present government is that people should stand on their own feet. Those claiming SB are not able to support themselves from earnings or personal savings; nor do national insurance or occupational pension benefits for which they may have contributed provide them with enough to meet even the basic SB level of requirements – they are, in short, unable to stand on their own feet. Since the Conservative government took office the number receiving SB has increased by about two-thirds, from about three million to nearly five million, as shown in diagram 1. When other members of recipients' families are included, *nearly eight million people (7,729,000) were dependent on SB in 1984, a massive increase of 77 per cent since 1979.* While incomes generally have risen by 14 per

22

Diagram 1: *Numbers on and below SB level*

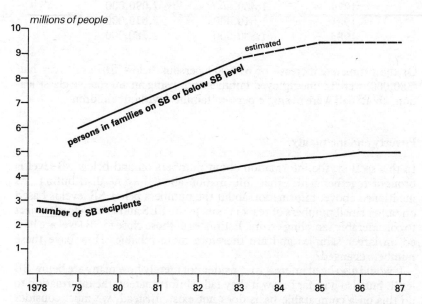

cent over the last eight years, three and a half million more people have become dependent on SB, at a level only 5 per cent above that of 1978.

The great majority of this increase is associated with increased unemployment, which has in the period far outstripped old age as the major characteristic of poverty: between 1979 and 1983 the number of people in unemployed families receiving SB tripled to 2.6 million, whereas the number over pension age fell slightly to 1.9 million. Between 1979 and 1983 the increased number of people in families dependent on SB was divided approximately equally between men, women and children, with about three-quarters of a million more of each. Extrapolating to 1987 suggests that *about one million more men, one million more women, and one million more children are now living at SB level than was the case in 1978.*

Numbers below SB level

While information on those in families receiving SB is extensive, evidence about those below SB level is extremely limited. What is available is based on analysis of the annual Family Expenditure Survey (FES). While later results are almost certainly available to the government, the latest published results relate only to 1983. The number of families and of persons with incomes *below* SB level was as follows:

	Families	Persons
1979	1,400,000	2,090,000
1981	1,610,000	2,610,000
1983	1,880,000	2,780,000

Of the estimated increase of 690,000 persons below SB level over half (380,000) were in unemployed families and, using an alternative classification, about half were in single person 'families' without children.

Poverty and inequality

In this section, the information about numbers on and below SB level is brought together with other information about income distribution. As mentioned above, information about the numbers below SB level is based on rather small numbers of respondents to the FES and is therefore subject to considerable sampling errors. Estimates of those close to SB level are based on larger samples and are therefore more reliable. How have these numbers changed?

It would also be of interest to consider not merely how many are below SB level, but also how far below it they fall. Unfortunately, the information to do this on a comparable basis does not exist. Instead, we must consider those who fall far below SB level in terms of material deprivation and physical insecurity – namely those who are homeless.

There is no doubt that the numbers with no fixed abode, sleeping rough with occasional nights in hostels, has greatly increased. George Orwell noted in *Down and Out in Paris and London* that this occurred in the 1930s, and observation in London confirms that it is occurring again fifty years later. However, there are not reliable statistics with which to measure this increase. Statistics are available on the numbers accepted by local authorities as 'homeless', the great majority of whom have experienced severe deprivation and stress; these include only a small number of homeless single people and childless couples, who have a very limited possibility of being accepted as 'homeless'. The increase in the number of official homeless is shown in diagram 2.

Also shown in the same diagram are the increases in those on and below SB level and the increase in the number close to poverty, defined here as those within 40 per cent of SB level. According to the DHSS, about 40 per cent of the increase in the total number in or close to poverty is attributable to the improvement in the real value of SB. This means, of course, that 60 per cent is not so attributable – that is, an increase of nearly three million people is unexplained. Further, it must be emphasised that this government attempt at exoneration is based on using a fixed absolute poverty level which represents a severely declining standard relative to overall income levels. What emerges is a picture of *increasing poverty regardless of the standard used*

Diagram 2: *The increase in poverty*

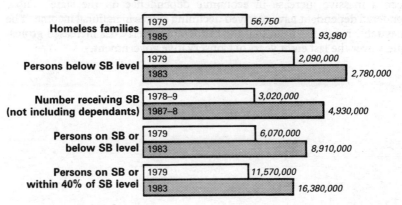

Homeless families	1979	56,750
	1985	93,980
Persons below SB level	1979	2,090,000
	1983	2,780,000
Number receiving SB (not including dependants)	1978–9	3,020,000
	1987–8	4,930,000
Persons on SB or below SB level	1979	6,070,000
	1983	8,910,000
Persons on SB or within 40% of SB level	1979	11,570,000
	1983	16,380,000

NB: drawn to scale but scales differ

to define poverty. The appropriate standard is open to argument and the adequacy of SB levels is itself open to question. But there can be no doubt that there has been a massive increase in the number left behind as the economy has grown. Thus, to the question 'Has economic growth given those at the bottom a constant or increasing share in the nation's income?', the answer is again a definite 'No'.

The increasing inequality in incomes is reflected in other government statistics, which show that between 1979 and 1985 both original and final incomes became more unequal. Not only have the numbers in poverty increased, but the gap between them and the better-off has widened, as chapter 4 demonstrates.

Conclusion

This chapter has concentrated on dependency on social security and on the financial circumstances of families. Many sources and forms of poverty have not been considered. For example, individual poverty may arise even within well-off households due to inequality in the distribution of resources within the family – on which no reliable data are available for any one year, let alone data to assess whether it has increased or not. Nor are financial circumstances the only measure of economic welfare. In important respects, as other chapters discuss, the period during which Mrs Thatcher has governed Britain has been one of growing economic insecurity for a substantial portion of the population. Savings, it is true, may be more secure against threats of inflation – but few of the poorest have any substantial savings, indeed problems of arrears and debts have been growing. Fears about unemployment and problems of coping on reduced income with the pressures of a society that is, overall, becoming more affluent have intensified.

Ironically, a government committed to economic independence has overseen a massive increase in economic dependence on the state. Those rendered dependent have received declining shares in national income. The inevitable result has been that the burden of poverty has increased grotesquely over the last eight years of Conservative government.

CHAPTER 4

Rich and poor: the growing divide

Dominic Byrne

The eight years since 1979 are years of increasingly sharp divisions. They are years during which the sales of champagne and Porsche motor cars have reached record levels at the same time as the numbers living in or close to poverty have increased significantly, as chapter 3 demonstrated. This chapter documents the effect of the Thatcher governments' policies on inequalities in pay, taxation, and the distribution of income and wealth.

Wages under the Conservatives

Government wage policy since 1979 has been characterised by two parallel and sharply contrasting attitudes. The first is a *laissez-faire* approach towards, and in some cases active encouragement of, rapid growth in the earnings of the high paid and many in the middle income brackets. On the other hand, the earnings of the low paid, and workers in the public sector, have been held down through a combination of deregulation of employment and wage protection, job schemes linked to low pay, public sector cash limits, and the straightforward fear of unemployment.

The promotion of a low wage economy as a motor for job creation and increased competitiveness has formed the central component of government economic policy. American economist J.K. Galbraith neatly summarised the perversity of such a policy: 'It holds that . . . the poor do not work because they have too much income; the rich do not work because they do not have enough income.'[1]

Since 1979 successive measures have been aimed at driving down the wages of the lower paid.

Cuts in employment rights

In 1979 and in the 1980 Employment Act, rights against unfair dismissal were made conditional on longer length of service, particularly for workers in small firms. The qualifying period was further extended in 1985, to two years for all full-time workers. Many part-time workers fail to qualify at all.

The Low Pay Unit estimates that around a third of the workforce is now disenfranchised from this basic employment right.[2] The lack of protection has undermined wage bargaining, particularly where trade union organisation is difficult. Indeed, the Policy Studies Institute found that, in 1984, half the workers in small firms failed to get a pay rise and many actually received pay cuts.[3]

Privatisation
In 1982 the government renounced the Fair Wages Resolution in order to open the door to widespread privatisation of public sector work without the requirement to make contractors subject to fair wage clauses. The effect has led to a downward spiralling of wages and conditions for already low paid workers in the civil service, the national health service and in some Conservative-controlled local authorities. In the civil service, for example, more than three-quarters of cleaners' jobs have been contracted out, resulting in wage cuts of between 10p and 35p on the already poor in-house rate of just £1.89 per hour.[4]

Young workers
In the youth labour market the government has promoted subsidies to employers to encourage low pay. Between 1981 and 1986 the Young Workers' Scheme and, more recently, the New Workers' Scheme have provided employers with a £15 weekly subsidy per job on condition that weekly wages for young workers are held below £55 and £65. Department of Employment surveys of employers participating in the scheme show that the effect has been to lower wages by as much as £20 per week, whilst having only a marginal effect on jobs.[5] Similar wage subsidies to encourage lower pay are now on offer to the long-term unemployed through the Jobstart scheme.

Minimum wage cuts
Wages council minimum wage protection, which until 1986 covered nearly 3 million workers in the service sector and low paid areas of manufacturing such as clothing, has been the most recent target of the government's deregulation policy. First weakened in 1979 through a cut of one-third in the number of wages inspectors, wages council protection was drastically reduced by the 1986 Wages Act. Half a million young workers, arguably the most vulnerable of all, were taken out of coverage altogether; while adult workers have seen the scope of protection and, in many cases, the level of wages council rates sharply reduced.[6]

The government has argued that such measures have been necessary in order to 'price workers into jobs'. It is a strategy that has been unsuccessful. When the Wages Bill was first introduced, Tom King, the then employment secretary, claimed that it would create between 50,000 and 100,000 new jobs.[7] It was a claim that was never repeated. Questioned recently about the effect on jobs, Kenneth Clarke and Lord Young admitted that it was impossible to make any job creation claims for the Wages Act.[8]

High pay and low pay: the widening divide

What *is* clear is that the government's policies, whilst unsuccessful in alleviating unemployment, have created record inequalities in earnings. Since 1979 the gap between the high paid and the low paid has widened into a huge gulf. So much so that the poorest workers are now markedly more worse off compared to higher earners than they were 100 years ago when pay statistics were first gathered:

- in 1886 manual workers in the bottom fifth of the pay ladder received 69 per cent of the average male manual wage;
- in 1986 wages in the bottom fifth of the manual distribution were worth only 65 per cent of the average;
- over the same period the top fifth in the manual pay league have moved upwards – from 43 per cent above the average to 55 per cent above.

For the low paid Margaret Thatcher's 'return to Victorian values' has become more than mere rhetoric.

But it is in the period since 1979 that the growth in pay inequality has been most dramatic. Over that period the proportion of the British workforce falling below the Council of Europe's minimum 'decency threshold' for wages increased from 36 per cent to 42.3 per cent (see chapter 5). Around 8.8 million workers earn less, excluding overtime, than the Council of Europe level (£125 per week in 1986/7).

Earnings for the high paid and middle income groups have, in contrast to the low paid, raced ahead. Table 1 shows the contrasting changes in earnings at different points on the earnings distribution.

Table 1: *Changes in the real level (adjusted for inflation) of gross earnings, April 1979 – April 1986*[9]

| Gross earnings (£ pwk) (constant 1986 prices) | | |
	April 1979	April 1986	% change
Lowest decile	107.40	111.40	+ 3.7
Median	166.40	185.10	+ 11.2
Highest decile	262.20	320.80	+ 22.3

Data is for male earnings, women's earnings follow a similar pattern.

The table shows the position of workers at the mid-point of the earnings distribution (median) and 10 percentage points from the two extremes of the distribution (the decile points). At the lowest decile there has been a small increase in gross earnings – £4 per week. In contrast, a wage-earner at the highest decile has seen earnings increase by over £58 – nearly 15 times the increase for the low paid.

Moreover, these figures mask the even poorer pay position of the low paid when set against price rises in earlier years. For much of the Thatcher years the earnings of the low paid failed even to keep up with inflation. Between 1979 and 1985, for example, the value of take-home earnings at the lowest decile point fell by 3 per cent – a real wage cut of £2.33 out of take-home pay in 1985 of just £80 per week.[10]

Worlds apart: the highest and the lowest paid
Even greater disparities in pay are evident at the two extremes of the earnings distribution. These are not documented in the Department of Employment's earnings survey. However, specific studies paint a picture of pay windfalls for top earners alongside pay cuts for those at the bottom. The financial services group Charterhouse, for example, reported in late 1986 that in just the six months up to August 1986 the average (median) director received a 10.2 per cent pay rise, but that a quarter of all directors received salary rises in excess of 16.7 per cent. The typical chairman or chief executive increased his earnings by 11.6 per cent in one year, yielding a midpoint on their salary ladder of £63,000.[11] Heading the pay ladder is the Burton Group's Ralph Halpern who, on top of his £1 million salary, also has the comfort of a £2½ million share option.

Meanwhile, at the bottom of the pay league, the minimum pay rates set by wages councils have been cut. The Wages Act has left those under 21 years old with no minimum rates at all. Many older workers have seen their rates cut. In hotel and catering, for example, the highest rate in 1986 was just £2.16 per hour. Now that has been cut to £1.85. For some workers in pubs and clubs the legal minimum rate has been reduced from £3.05 to £2.07.

Outside the wages council sector many low paid workers have received cuts in real wage levels. A study of civil service pay by the Low Pay Unit showed that pay for low paid grades such as cleaners and security officers had fallen in real terms by 4.4 per cent since 1980. Compared to workers in the economy as a whole, these grades were up to £20 a week worse off. On top of this, cuts in housing benefit meant that living standards had been cut in total by as much as £30 per week.[12]

Taxation under the Conservatives

The earnings gap that has grown in the Thatcher years has been widened even further as a result of government tax policy. About 6½ million taxpayers – nearly one in three – have an income of less than £125 per week. They include most families considered poor enough to claim family income supplement. Despite Margaret Thatcher's publicly stated concern that those on low incomes are paying too much tax, the poorest have gained little from tax cuts since 1979. Out of the £8.1 billion given away in tax cuts between 1979 and 1986:

- the poorest 6 million taxpayers received only 8 per cent (most of this has been outweighed by increased national insurance payments);
- one-fifth went to the richest 1 per cent;
- one-third went to the richest 5 per cent;
- nearly half went to the richest 10 per cent and almost two-thirds went to the richest 20 per cent.[13]

The effect of this highly unequal division of the budget spoils has been to provide astonishingly large tax windfalls to the highly paid whilst leaving most average and low wage-earners with higher overall tax burdens. Following the 1986 budget the *Daily Telegraph* reported on celebrations in wine bars throughout the City – 'nowhere was post-Budget euphoria greater this week than among the young men of the City.'[14] The breakdown of tax cuts between 1979 and 1987 explains the continuing cause for celebration among the rich:

- taxpayers with incomes over £50,000 a year – just 0.7 per cent of all taxpayers – received 15 per cent of the total spent on income tax cuts, giving them an average tax cut worth £11,400 per year, or £219 per week;
- at the other end of the scale, 3.2 million taxpayers with incomes below £5,000 per year – nearly one in six of all taxpayers – received less than 3 per cent of income tax cuts, giving them an average tax cut of just £85 per year, or £1.63 each week.

Table 2 shows in detail where the tax cuts have gone. It looks at income tax alone. When national insurance contributions are also taken into account, the small reduction in income tax for ordinary and low paid taxpayers

Table 2: *Where the tax cuts have gone*
1987/88 compared with 1978/79[15]

Range of total income in 1987/88	Nos of units paying tax in 1987/88 (m)	Reductions in income tax compared with 1978/79 indexed regime	
		Amount £m	Av per tax unit £
Under £5,000	3.20	350	85
£5,000-10,000	7.60	1,950	250
£10,000-15,000	5.30	2,550	480
£15,000-20,000	2.70	1,950	710
£20,000-30,000	1.60	2,000	1,240
£30,000-50,000	0.60	1,450	2,380
Over £50,000	0.15	1,750	11,400
Total	21.2	12,000	540

disappears completely. Instead, taking income tax and national insurance together, the direct tax burden faced by most low and average income households has risen – in some cases, as table 3 shows, it has doubled.

Overall, only one in seven employed taxpayers was paying a smaller proportion of his/her income in direct taxes in 1986/7 compared with seven years earlier. For a small number of the very low paid the introduction of reduced rate bands of national insurance contributions had reduced the burden of direct taxation slightly. But the vast majority of gainers were concentrated in the higher income brackets – above £15,600 per annum.[16]

It was not until after the 1987 budget that tax cuts began to reach down even to the middle earnings bracket. For the first time since 1980 the burden of direct taxation on average earners began to fall below its 1978/79 level. The fall, though, was marginal and did little to make up for earlier years. Moreover, it was not a fall that reached most of those on below

Table 3: *Shifting the tax burden*[17]

Income tax and NI contributions (less child benefit where appropriate) as proportion of earnings, 1978/79 to 1987/88

	Multiple of average male earnings*				
	½×	1×	2×	5×	10×
Single					
1978/79	23.5	31.5	33.7	52.2	67.4
1982/83	27.3	33.0	34.5	45.9	53.0
1986/87	25.8	31.9	33.3	45.7	52.8
1987/88	25.1	30.5	32.2	45.9	53.0
Overall change	+7%	−3%	−4%	−12%	−21%
Married (no children)					
1978/79	16.0	27.8	31.4	50.5	66.5
1982/83	20.8	29.8	32.3	44.6	52.3
1986/87	18.9	28.5	30.9	44.2	52.1
1987/88	18.9	27.4	29.7	44.6	52.3
Overall change	+18%	−1%	−5%	−12%	−21%
Married (two children)					
1978/79	2.4	20.8	27.9	48.8	65.6
1982/83	6.9	22.8	28.8	43.2	51.6
1986/87	5.7	21.8	27.6	42.9	51.5
1987/88	6.3	21.1	26.5	43.3	51.6
Overall change	+163%	+1%	−5%	−11%	−21%

* Average male earnings are estimated at £230 in 1987/88 (derived from the Treasury's 1986/87 level, uprated by average earnings increase in the Department of Employment *Gazette*).

32

average earnings and households with children. Instead, the most needy taxpayers continue to face higher burdens of taxation under the Conservatives – in stark contrast to the gains of the better-off. Table 3 shows how tax burdens have fallen for the rich and risen for the poor.

The 1987 budget

The 1987 budget consolidated the Chancellor's leading contribution to a divided Britain. The budget failed to contain a single measure aimed at the problem of unemployment. Instead, £2.7 billion was spent on cutting the basic rate of tax by 2p. Evidence from the economic models used by the Treasury and the Bank of England shows that this amount of money, if used to boost government expenditure, could have resulted in the creation of between 270,000 and 415,000 new jobs.[18]

For those liable to income tax, the 2p reduction continued the pattern of unequal tax cuts established in earlier budgets. For the poor, the 2p cut was more than swallowed up by a 3p increase in the housing benefit means-test. For the low paid who escape this poverty trap, the tax cut remained of little value – worth just 84p to someone on half average male earnings. In contrast, at twice average earnings, the tax cut was worth £6.88 – more than eight times as much.

In richness and in wealth

Income tax cuts and high earnings increases have not been the only cause for celebration of the Thatcher government's policies among the better-off in recent years. Successive budgets have contained a number of measures designed to provide further concessions to the wealthy. These measures provide the icing on a very rich tax cut cake from successive Conservative Chancellors.

The 1984 budget, for example, scrapped the investment income surcharge. Again, it was a tax measure that was strictly for the benefit of the better-off. The spread of investment income is far more unequal than that of earned income. In 1983/84, the most recent period for which figures are available, 24 per cent of earned income was received by those with total incomes above £15,000 per annum. In contrast, the proportion of total income from investments going to this high income group was 43.9 per cent.[19]

At the time of the 1984 budget the Chancellor claimed that investment income surcharge was particularly unfair on the elderly. In fact, people would have had to have accumulated savings in excess of £100,000 to be liable for the surcharge at all. Even then, their investment income would still have been taxed less heavily than the equivalent amount of income from earnings.[20]

The 1986 budget alone contained three major announcements which further enhanced the government's aggrandisement of the better-off. Capital

33

transfer tax was abolished altogether on lifetime gifts (except those made in the last few years of life), stamp duty on share transactions was halved and personal equity plans, a new form of tax-free savings for the wealthy, were introduced. The cost of these three measures was estimated at £155 million – around three times the amount spent in that year on the 10p increase in child benefit.

The rich were not disappointed by the 1987 budget either. While the starting level for income tax was raised by 3.7 per cent, the Chancellor felt it necessary to raise the threshold for capital transfer tax (now renamed inheritance tax) by 27 per cent – from £71,000 to £90,000. This was a measure perhaps designed for the less well-advised holder of wealth, since any decent accountant would be able to find enough loopholes in the inheritance tax to pass on wealth far in excess of the nominal threshold completely tax free.

Divided welfare: Britain's two welfare states

The effect of the government's taxation policies has been to reinforce the sharpest increase in inequality recorded in modern times. Only the welfare protection constructed after the Second World War has stood between 1980s' Britain and the deep extremes of Victorian and depression era poverty. However, as demonstrated in chapters 3, 9 and 10, benefit provision, inadequate though it has proved to be in many respects, has itself been cut back by the government since 1979.

Social security provision for the working poor and the elderly has come under particular attack. Successive reductions in the scope of the housing benefit scheme have meant that 1.4 million low paid and pensioner households have lost help with rent and rates altogether. The elderly have suffered a double blow with the repeal in 1980 of the legal requirement to increase pensions and other long-term benefits in line with earnings whenever they rose faster than prices.

At the same time, increasingly large amounts of government revenue is foregone, in effect spent, on subsidies for mortgage interest payments and private pension provision. These 'tax expenditures' are the main pillars of the 'fiscal welfare state'. The benefits from this spending are means-tested. But, unlike means-tested social security, tax relief on private pensions and mortgage interest *increases* as incomes rise.

Because they are linked to tax rates, the subsidy from reliefs is worth more than twice as much to top rate taxpayers as to the mass of basic rate taxpayers. This extreme regressive effect is compounded both by the exclusion of those who are too poor to pay tax and inequalities in income which limit access by the poor to house purchase and pension ownership. Indeed, in 1985/86 over a third of the money spent on mortgage relief, for example, went to the top 2 per cent of taxpayers.[21]

There is common ground between a wide range of political and academic opinion that these 'tax expenditures' exert a damaging influence. Besides their obvious effect in reinforcing inequality, they create perverse distortions in investment and housing markets. In spite of this, successive governments of different political persuasions have fought shy of dismantling the tax relief structure. Instead, under the present government tax expenditures have consumed expanding amounts of public spending at the expense of the social security system:

● annual expenditure on mortgage relief and approved pension schemes alone was nearly £3.4 billion higher in real terms in 1985/86 compared with 1978/79;[22]
● in contrast, in the same year, the government made a saving of £2.2 billion as a result of cuts in the social security budget since 1979.[23]

Wealth and incomes: the growing divide

Wealth
The trends identified in earnings, taxes and benefits are reflected in patterns of income and wealth distribution. Until the late 1970s there had been a long-term trend towards a marginal redistribution of wealth. However, this historical trend was from the very rich to the rich, rather than from rich to poor. Redistribution since the inter-war period failed to reach much beyond the top 20 per cent. During the Thatcher years, however, even that small amount of redistribution has been halted. The clear effect of current government policy has been to buttress existing extremes of wealth. In 1984:

● over half (52 per cent) of all personal marketable wealth was owned by the richest 10 per cent;
● more than a fifth (21 per cent) of personal marketable wealth was concentrated in the hands of the richest 1 per cent;
● in stark contrast, the bottom 50 per cent of the population controlled just 7 per cent of marketable wealth.

Even if the definition of wealth is widened to allow for occupational and state pension rights, 79-83 per cent of wealth remains controlled by the richest half of the nation. Translating these patterns into individual sums brings wealth inequality into even sharper focus. The average wealth holding in the top 1 per cent was £375,000 in 1984 – 150 times the average £2,500 per head for those in the bottom 50 per cent.

Income
Income is more evenly distributed than wealth. However, the Thatcher government has presided over a sharp 'negative' redistribution of income, in favour of those already on high incomes. Mass unemployment, together with the increased inequality produced by the interaction of government policy on wages, taxes, benefits and wealth, has meant that:

35

- the proportion of original income received by the poorest fifth of households in 1985 had fallen to little more than a third of its 1979 level – the result largely of the growth of unemployment;
- the original income share of the poorest 40 per cent had fallen by more than a third – reflecting the combined effect of unemployment and low pay;
- in contrast, the top fifth of households had seen their income share rise by an average of 10 per cent.

'Original' income is used to describe income from non-government sources – from employment, occupational pensions, investments and gifts. 'Disposable income' is a measure of income after the effects of state benefits and payments of income tax and national insurance are taken into account. 'Final income' refers to 'disposable income' after the payment of indirect taxes, such as rates and VAT, and the receipt of imputed benefits of government spending on services, such as health and education.

Table 4: *Distribution of total household income, 1976-85* [24]

	Share of income by household group (%)			
	Bottom fifth	Bottom 40%	Top 40%	Top fifth
Original income				
1976	0.8	10.2	71.0	44.4
1981	0.6	8.7	73.3	46.4
1983	0.3	7.0	75.2	48.0
1985	0.3	6.3	76.0	49.0
% change in income share				
1976-85	−63%	−38%	+7%	+10%
Disposable income				
1976	7.0	19.6	62.2	38.1
1981	6.7	18.8	63.5	39.4
1983	6.9	18.8	63.6	39.6
1985	6.5	17.5	65.0	41.0
% change in income share				
1976-85	−7%	−11%	+5%	+8%
Final income				
1976	7.4	20.1	61.9	37.9
1981	7.1	19.5	62.6	38.6
1983	6.9	19.1	63.3	39.3
1985	6.7	18.7	64.0	40.0
% change in income share				
1976-85	−9%	−7%	+3%	+6%

Social security benefits and spending on government services helps the lower income groups. Even so, the distribution of final income remains highly unequal. The top fifth still command twice the share of income suggested by their population size. The poorest 20 per cent of households receive less than 7 per cent of total final income.

Between 1979 and 1985 inequality in both disposable and final income grew wider:

- the top 20 per cent increased their share of disposable income by 8 per cent, with final income rising by 6 per cent;
- the poorest 20 per cent of households saw their share of disposable income fall by 7 per cent, with final income falling by 9 per cent.

Table 4 charts the growth of income inequality during the first six years of Thatcher government.

Cashing in on inequality

At the centre of current Conservative orthodoxy is the promotion of the 'enterprise' culture. Many ministers now make no secret of the role of greater inequality within government policy. Employment minister Lord Young, for example, drawing a proud parallel with Victorian entrepreneurs, has said that 'we need not feel guilty that their success was at the expense of the poor.'[25]

The spin-offs from the promotion of 'enterprise' and 'popular capitalism' have reinforced the growth in inequality. Share give-aways, tax perk saving schemes, and the boom in South-east house prices have had the effect of leaving the poor further behind. 'Yuppies' can cash in, but the great mass of the poor are left out in the cold.

The aggrandisement of those with money to invest has been boosted by large outpourings of government spending. Most spectacular has been the flotation of shares in publicly owned companies. Virtually every flotation has provided a substantial profit for those with the money to take advantage of the government's give-aways. In total, adding up the undervaluation of privatised concerns and the huge publicity costs and brokers fees, the government has spent around £2.9 billion on the privatisation programme.[26] That's more than half of total spending on child benefit in the whole of 1986/87.

Those with enough money to make a fast buck by buying £5,000 worth of shares in each of the flotations and selling immediately would have added £12,500 to their wealth (this is an illustrative example – oversubscription of some share offers limited buyers to less than £5,000). In addition, there has been no shortage of other less spectacular, but still heavily subsidised, money-spinners for the better-off. These include the business expansion scheme, personal equity plans and, the Chancellor's latest favourite, profit-related pay.

Conclusion: future trends

In many respects we are seeing only the first effects of Thatcherite policies on income and wealth inequalities. Even with a change of government, the legacy of many of the measures of the past eight years will still feed through in future years. But what if current Tory policy is continued?

Two time-bombs are ticking away, set to widen even further the gap between the rich and the poor. First, there are the changes made to pensions by the 1986 Social Security Act. In addition, the earlier abandonment of the link between pensions and earnings will cut the value of the basic pension by more than half in the next half century, even on the government's rather conservative assumption of 1 per cent annual earnings growth.[27]

Booming house and property prices, particularly in London and the South-east, represent the second time-bomb. This boom is set to produce a 'new wealth'. Greater regional inequality and housing crisis are the obvious results. Its effects go further, though, as Neal Ascherson has described in the *Observer*. Writing about 'London's new class', Ascherson points out that the, largely unfettered, effect of inherited property wealth will mean that 'in the next decade or so the upward-mobile classes of London will acquire staggering reserves of liquid cash'. He writes:

> This will mean a return to degrees of inequality unknown in Britain for a hundred years. A segregation as blatant as that of apartheid is approaching, founded on inequality of wealth but built up into an entirely separate way of life in separate institutions.[29]

The disintegration of manufacturing and organised labour and its partial replacement with service sector-led low paid employment has produced a new 'servant class' alongside but, in economic terms, far apart from the emerging 'new wealthy'.

If the Conservatives are successful at the polls, their plans for a third term will hasten these developments. The full implementation of the Social Security Act will accompany further measures to deregulate the labour market. On the public agenda so far are moves to dismantle national pay bargaining at the expense of the poorer regions, the contracting-out of local government services to low paying contractors, and a further dismantling of employment rights, particularly those of part-time women workers.

Too controversial to put on the public agenda are further moves to penalise the unemployed for refusal to take low paid work. The recent focus of employment ministers on the 'availability for work' rules and the implementation of the Restart scheme suggest that they would not be averse to more compulsory measures if returned with a comfortable majority. At the other end of the income scale, ministers have made clear their desire to continue the tax bonanza for the wealthy by cutting the top rates of tax. Another Conservative government, in the same mould as the last two, would see the further widening of the gulf in income and wealth between rich and poor and the consolidation of these two nations of haves and have-nots.

CHAPTER 5

Divided Britain

Steve Winyard

This chapter is about a divided Britain; a divided not a united Kingdom. The main focus is on divisions between regions. Broadly speaking, since 1979 the South has prospered and the North has been allowed to decline. A wide gap has opened up between the 'two nations', and only concerted government action can hope to reverse the process. However, just as important are divisions within regions. Within the North and within the South, within each region, city and town, the gap between the poor and the prosperous is becoming a gulf. As *Faith in the City* observed:

> rich and poor, suburban and inner city, privileged and deprived, have been becoming more sharply separated from each other for many years and . . . the impoverished minority has become increasingly cut off from the mainstream of our national life. . . . These trends add up to a pattern warranting the label of polarisation in a new, comprehensive and intractable form.[1]

In this chapter we start by looking briefly at population change within each region – the South-east, for example, which contains nearly one-third of the population of the United Kingdom, grew by a little under 1 per cent between 1979 and 1984; the poorer areas of 'the North', in contrast, experienced a fall in population.

The second section focuses on unemployment, and looks both at the clear North/South divide, and at the very unequal distribution *within* regions. The duration of unemployment, which widens further the inequality between the North and the South, is also considered. Finally, this section summarises the main conclusions of an unpublished government report recently submitted to the European Commission. This indicates that the government does not expect regional differences in unemployment to narrow by 1990. However, the report also shows clearly that the government knows how significantly to reduce regional unemployment but that it chooses not to take action.

The third section of this chapter focuses on the rapid widening of pay inequalities between and within regions since 1979. Government policies have been highly successful in holding down the wages of the low paid, with workers in areas of high unemployment tending to come off worst.

The final section looks at the distribution of poverty between regions. Unfortunately, the government does not consider the issue to be of sufficient importance to produce any figures, so a number of indirect indicators must be used. Here we examine the proportion of household income derived from social security benefits, the numbers of children receiving free school meals, and data on regional income from the Family Expenditure Survey (FES). All of these confirm the impoverishment of the North.

Population change

Between 1979 and 1984 the total population of the UK grew by 0.5 per cent. However, as can be seen from table 1, there were sharp differences between regions. Broadly speaking, it was the more prosperous areas that grew and the poorer areas that experienced a fall in population. East Anglia had the highest growth rate of 4.1 per cent, whilst at the other extreme the population of the North-west contracted by 1.6 per cent. The most obvious exception to this pattern was Northern Ireland. Despite having the highest levels of unemployment and poverty in the UK, its population grew by 1.7 per cent.

Table 1: *Population of the standard region*[2]

	Total population (000s)	Population change 1979-84 %
South-east	17,112	0.9
North-east	6,395	-1.6
West Midlands	5,176	-0.1
Yorkshire & Humberside	4,904	-0.3
South-west	4,461	2.9
East Midlands	3,874	1.5
North	3,093	-1.2
East Anglia	1,940	4.1
Scotland	5,146	-0.4
Wales	2,807	-0.1
Northern Ireland	1,578	1.7
United Kingdom	56,488	0.5

Differences *within* regions are, however, just as important as differences *between* regions. Within the massive South-east region there was far greater variation in rates of population change than in the country as a whole. Whilst Greater London experienced a 1.9 per cent loss of population,

Buckinghamshire grew by 7.6 per cent and Berkshire, with its concentration of 'sunrise' new technology industry, by 4.9 per cent. Even within the North-west region, which faced the most rapid contraction in population, there were areas of growth. Between 1979 and 1984 the population of Cheshire increased by 1.0 per cent, due in part to the movement of more affluent households out of Manchester and Merseyside. These two conurbations, with their high levels of unemployment and inner area decay, experienced rates of population decline of 2.0 and 3.4 per cent respectively.

Unemployment

Unemployment statistics provide one of the clearest indicators that the United Kingdom is, in fact, a divided kingdom. Looking first at the regional figures, table 2 shows that there is a remarkably clear North-South divide. At the beginning of 1987 both the Northern region and Northern Ireland had unemployment running at twice the level in the South-east. Scotland was not far behind (15.1 per cent), whilst the North-west, Yorkshire and Humberside, and the West Midlands were all significantly above the national average.

Table 2: *Regional unemployment, January 1987* [3]

	% of working population registered unemployed
North	16.9
North-west	14.3
Yorkshire & Humberside	13.8
West Midlands	13.8
East Midlands	11.4
South-west	10.4
East Anglia	9.3
South-east	8.5
Northern Ireland	19.3
Scotland	15.1
Wales	14.3
United Kingdom	11.9

These figures, however, disguise the full extent of inequality in the distribution of unemployment. Within each of the regions certain communities have been far more seriously affected than others. At the beginning of 1987 there were 18 towns and cities in England ('travel-to-work areas') that had an official unemployment rate of over 20 per cent. As might be expected, six were in the Northern region; Bishop Auckland (20.0 per cent),

41

Alnwick and Amble (20.4 per cent), Sunderland (21.4 per cent), Middles-borough (22.2 per cent), Hartlepool (23.2 per cent) and South Tyneside (25.9 per cent). However, there were also areas in the same region with unemployment below 10 per cent. Indeed, Kendal had only 8.3 per cent of its workforce out of a job, less than half the average for the North.

The South-west was the area of greatest contrast.[4] Despite having an overall unemployment rate below the national average, it contained five of the 18 travel-to-work areas in England with more than 20 per cent unemployment. One of these areas, Newquay, had the highest level of unemployment in England at the beginning of 1987 (28.1 per cent). It should be noted, however, that the five areas are all dependent to a signifi-cant extent on tourism, and enjoy somewhat lower levels of unemployment in the summer. At the other extreme are areas such as Cheltenham (7.4 per cent), Salisbury (8.7 per cent) and Bath (8.9 per cent), with less than one in 10 of the population out of work.

In Wales, Scotland and Northern Ireland there is rather less variation around generally high levels of unemployment. At the beginning of 1987, seven out of 35 travel-to-work areas in Wales had unemployment rates of over 20 per cent. Most seriously affected were Cardigan (26.2 per cent) and Lampeter and Aberaeron (25.0 per cent). In Scotland 16 out of 60 travel-to-work areas had unemployment rates of over the 20 per cent mark, including many of the ship-building towns such as Girvan (26.4 per cent), Irvine (26.3 per cent) and Greenock (21.4 per cent). Also high up in this listing was Bathgate (22.0 per cent), the victim of government policies for the motor in-dustry. Finally, in Northern Ireland 10 out of 12 areas had more than one in five people out of work. Indeed, five towns had over 30 per cent unemployed at the beginning of 1987, with Strabane topping the list with 39.1 per cent.

Winchester and Strabane
At the two extremes of the divided kingdom are Winchester in Hampshire and Strabane in Northern Ireland. The former has an unemployment rate of 5.2 per cent, the latter 39.1 per cent. They both have, however, a very similar *number* of people out of work; 3,925 in Winchester, and 3,957 in Strabane. The position and prospects of these people could not be more dif-ferent. For those in Winchester finding a job is a realistic prospect. Unemployment is largely a short-term problem, with few people out of work for more than a month or so. In Strabane unemployment is endemic and long-term. The realist stops looking for work; there is an 'unemployed community' in which poverty and deprivation are sharply concentrated.

Long-term unemployment
These 'snapshot' figures, however, seriously understate the extent of inequality between and within regions, since they ignore the duration of unemployment. Not only is unemployment far higher in the North, but also

people stay on the register for longer periods. At the beginning of 1987 arouind *half* of all unemployed men in the North (47.9 per cent), North-west (48.7 per cent), Yorkshire and Humberside (46.3 per cent), and West Midlands (50.7 per cent) had been out of work for more than a year. In Northern Ireland the proportion was as high as 56 per cent. This compares with just under 40 per cent in the South-east, 36.8 per cent in East Anglia and 35.9 per cent in the South-west.

Long-term unemployment appears to be a less serious problem amongst women than men. Around one-third of unemployed women in the 'northern' regions had been out of work for over a year, and a little over one-quarter in the South-east, East Anglia and South-west. However, these generally lower figures reflect the significant discrimination in the registration and benefits system, together with the growth of low paid 'female' part-time employment. They certainly do not indicate a markedly more favourable labour market position.

Bleak prospects

Unfortunately, there is no prospect of improvement in this gross employment imbalance between the North and the South without major changes in both macro-economic and regional policy. As the recent 17-volume report to the European Commission, *UK Regional Development Programme 1986–1990*, shows, the government has projected that employment will still be above 3 million in 1990, and that there will be no change in the current regional unemployment differential.

Focussing on the regions which currently face high unemployment, the report describes the prospects as 'frighteningly bleak', 'not encouraging' and 'gloomy'.

● In the case of the North-east the report admits that unemployment is the major problem facing the area. It argues that 'the situation will not improve until a number of other more fundamental problems are resolved', and refers specifically to a weak economic structure, an inadequate infrastructure, environmental dereliction and social deprivation.

● In the West Midlands there is 'little prospect of an improvement in the region's basic unemployment problem'. Six major constraints to future development are identified, including 'the cumulative effect of under-investment in apprenticeships and in modern plant and machinery'.

● The report on the North-west region speaks of 'the growing disparity between the availability of jobs and the number seeking jobs'. The prospects in the Greater Merseyside sub-region are 'frighteningly bleak' with outmoded transport facilities unsuited to modern demands, and decay and obsolescence in much of the basic infrastructure. In Greater Manchester a further increase in unemployment 'seems to be the most likely prospect', and again reference is made to 'major infrastructure problems'.

● In the Humberside region unemployment, already high, is predicted to rise further. Similarly, in South and West Yorkshire future economic prospects are 'not encouraging'.[5] A legacy of ageing infrastructure and many obsolete industrial buildings have 'a depressing effect on private investment'. Diversification is called for to reduce dependence on traditional and declining industries.

● Industrial South Wales is 'beset by grave economic problems. During the 1980s there has been a continuing shedding of labour in steel, coal and in the manufacturing sector.' Further job losses are predicted. Whilst some bright spots are noted, particularly electronics, 'the scale of the remaining problem – high unemployment, extremely so at certain localities, – is vast'.

● Scotland is also likely to face further job losses in steel, coal mining and ship building. Like Wales, there has been some success in attracting electronics and other technology based industries. Overall, however, there is 'little possibility of sufficient expansion in the economy to reduce unemployment significantly in the next few years'.

A consistent theme in the report is the harmful effect that inadequate public expenditure is having on depressed regional economies. This is most clearly expressed in the volume on the North-west: 'Continuing restraint on public expenditure will directly constrain employment in public services and indirectly employment in the private sector.' Similarly, the West Midlands volume argues that tight controls on public expenditure prevent public authorities from taking advantage of significant infrastructure development opportunities. 'This in turn limits employment arising from construction programmes and major capital projects.' Again, in the North-east development of the regional economy is held back by 'continuing restraint on public expenditure, restricting direct employment in public services and indirect employment arising from public investment'.

The message is clear. A great deal could be done to bring down regional unemployment. However, the government has chosen to give tax cuts to those in work, rather than focus resources on job-creating public sector capital projects and improved public services. By the government's own admission, the result will be further rises in regional unemployment and a worsening of the already serious infrastructure problems.

Widening pay inequalities

Alongside the growth in unemployment there has been a marked increase in pay inequalities. As we saw in chapter 4, the gap between the high paid and low paid nationally widened to an unprecedented extent between 1979 and 1986. A major factor contributing to this has been the much faster growth of earnings in the South-east compared to the depressed 'North'. In table 3 average earnings in the regions in 1979 and 1986 are shown as a percentage of the corresponding average for the South-east. In all cases,

Table 3: *Regional earnings of full-time workers,*
1979 and 1986[6]

| | Average earnings as a percentage of South-east average | | | |
| | 1979 | | 1986 | |
Region	Men	Women	Men	Women
South-east	100.0	100.0	100.0	100.0
East Anglia	88.4	88.0	83.8	83.6
South-west	85.2	87.0	82.9	83.7
West Midlands	90.4	89.8	83.3	82.4
East Midlands	89.5	87.3	82.0	81.7
Yorkshire &				
Humberside	91.3	86.8	83.0	82.2
North-west	91.4	88.4	85.2	85.0
North	91.9	88.6	82.8	83.3
Wales	90.0	89.8	81.8	82.6
Scotland	93.3	88.3	86.5	84.4

there has been a widening of the pay differential. However, it has tended to be the areas with the highest levels of unemployment that have experienced the largest falls in relative pay. Earnings of men in the North, for example, fell over the period by more than 9 per cent compared to those in the South-east. Yorkshire and Humberside is another area that has experienced a rapid increase in unemployment since 1979, and here relative earnings of men have fallen by 8.3 per cent. In the case of women the changes have been somewhat smaller, but again it is the areas of high unemployment that have tended to come off worst.

The rich get richer

Not only has the overall pay gap between the North and the South widened, but inequalities *within* regions have also increased sharply. For example, in Yorkshire and Humberside in 1979 'high paid' men (on highest decile earnings) were receiving 152 per cent of the regional average whilst the low paid (on lowest decile earnings) were on 66 per cent. By 1986 the respective figures were 162 per cent and 60 per cent. Similarly, in the case of women in Yorkshire and Humberside the low paid fell from 71 per cent to 68 per cent of the average, and the high paid rose from 158 per cent to 173 per cent.

This pattern is repeated across the regions, including the South-east, and is evidence of the success of the government's 'two nations' policy in the area of pay. As was discussed in chapter 4, unemployment, together with the weakening of the wages council system, the abolition of the Fair Wages Resolution, privatisation and a discriminatory public sector pay policy, have all helped to hold down the wages of the low paid. Indeed, the 1980s have seen certain groups amongst the low paid experiencing pay cuts – the first time that this has happened since the 1930s.

Twice as big
The increase in the regional low pay problem between 1979 and 1986 can be seen in table 4, where the Council of Europe's 'decency threshold' for wages as the definition of low pay (68 per cent of average (mean) earnings of men and women) is used. This gives a figure of £60 per week in 1979 and £125 per week in 1986.

Table 4: *Low pay in the regions, 1979 and 1986*[7]

	1979 % of full-time workers earning less than £60		1986 % of full-time workers earning less than £125	
	men	women	men	women
South-east	6.4	41.8	11.8	37.9
East Anglia	10.7	59.3	17.7	56.8
South-west	11.8	60.5	19.1	57.8
West Midlands	7.0	56.6	16.8	59.1
East Midlands	8.4	59.8	18.3	60.6
Yorkshire & Humberside	8.6	61.0	18.4	59.6
North-west	8.7	58.2	17.5	55.8
North	8.1	60.2	17.3	59.2
Wales	9.9	56.8	19.7	58.1
Scotland	9.3	59.5	18.9	58.3

As can be seen, in all regions there was a sharp increase in the proportion of the male workforce receiving low wages. The rise was smallest in the South-east, East Anglia and the South-west (although East Anglia and the South-west started the period with the most serious low pay problems). In all other regions the low pay problem amongst men more than doubled between 1979 and 1986.

For women workers there was little change in a much more serious problem. With the exception of the South-east, approximately 60 per cent of women workers in each of the regions were low paid in 1979. By 1986 the situation had improved marginally in East Anglia, the South-west, Yorkshire and Humberside, the North-west, the North and Scotland. However, in the Midlands there was a slight increase in the low pay problem.

Poverty in the regions

The growth in unemployment and low pay since 1979 has had a major impact on poverty in Britain. As we saw in chapter 3, the number of people living on what the DHSS defines as a low income increased by 42 per cent between 1979 and 1983 (while about two-fifths of this increase is attributed

46

to a rise in the real value of the supplementary benefit benchmark, three-fifths is not so attributable). When the figures for 1985 and 1987 are eventually published they will undoubtedly show a further increase.

The problem is, of course, much greater in areas of high unemployment and low wages. Unfortunately, the government does not consider the issue to be of sufficient importance to produce statistics of poverty by region.

However, there are some indirect indicators which confirm that deprivation is not spread evenly across the country. It *is* concentrated in the North, the North-west, the West Midlands, Wales and Scotland. Again, *within* the regions poverty is not spread evenly. It is concentrated in the 'unemployed communities' where more than a fifth of the workforce is out of a job; in the decaying inner areas of towns and cities such as Liverpool, Manchester, Birmingham, Bradford, Sunderland and Glasgow; and in the massive council estates built in the 1950s and 1960s to solve the inner-city problem. Finally, it must be remembered that even in the more prosperous South-east, East Anglia and South-west there are large numbers of people living in poverty due to low wages and the inadequacies of the social security system.

The first indicator of the increase in poverty since 1979 is the growing dependence of certain regions on social security benefits as a source of income. As can be seen from table 5, in the North, Wales and Northern Ireland around one-fifth of household incomes is accounted for by social security benefits.

Table 5: *Regional dependence on social security benefits,*
1979/80– 1983/4 [8]

	% of gross household income from social security benefits	
	1979/80	1983/84
South-east	9.4	9.7
East Anglia	11.0	15.1
South-west	14.2	13.2
East Midlands	10.8	13.5
West Midlands	11.1	15.0
Yorkshire & Humberside	15.1	16.7
North-west	14.0	17.0
North	15.7	20.0
Wales	15.5	19.5
Scotland	12.6	17.1
Northern Ireland	19.3	23.6

In the West Midlands, Yorkshire and Humberside, and the North-west, benefits account for approximately one-sixth of regional household income.

Given this sort of dependency, the level of social security benefits is of vital importance to the local economy. Improvements could make a significant contribution to boosting economic activity and employment.

A second indicator of the existence of 'two nations' in Britain is the proportion of children taking free school meals. In October 1984 it varied from around a quarter in Yorkshire and Humberside (23.5 per cent), the North-west (24.5 per cent), the North (25.4 per cent), and Northern Ireland (28.0 per cent), the South-east (12.2 per cent) and the South-west (12.4 per cent).

A final indicator of the growing divide between the prosperous South-east and the impoverished North is actual household income. Data from the recently published 1985 Family Expenditure Survey (FES) shows that, overall, average weekly household income in the North (£170.40) was little more than two-thirds that in the South-east in 1984-5 (£248). Six years earlier average income in the North was about four-fifths of that in the South-east. Similarly, incomes in the West Midlands have fallen sharply, from 87 per cent of the South-east level in 1979/82 to 77 per cent in 1984/5.

Table 6: *Regional income, 1979/80– 1984/5* [9]

	Average weekly household income		% of households with income below £100
	1979/80 £	1984/85 £	1984/85 %
South-east	153.2	248.0	22.3
East Anglia	131.0	204.8	32.2
South-west	124.2	208.8	25.8
East Midlands	135.4	203.2	28.0
West Midlands	133.5	192.4	30.0
Yorkshire & Humberside	116.7	179.1	35.7
North-west	128.0	183.2	34.6
North	119.3	170.4	37.6
Wales	124.0	187.1	32.3
Scotland	126.5	198.3	32.2
Northern Ireland	113.0	172.9	37.1

The final column in table 6 shows the proportion of households in each region in 1984/85 with an income of less than £100 per week (slightly less than half average income in the UK in 1984/85 – £206.75). Whilst the data is not related to household size, it does show a clear North/South gradient in low income. Just over 20 per cent of households in the South-east had an income of less than half the national average in 1984/85. In the North and Northern Ireland the proportion was approximately 40 per cent.

Conclusion

Over the past eight years the government has allowed the United Kingdom to become a divided kingdom. The gap between the rich and the poor has further opened up not only *between* regions but *within* regions.

Increased unemployment, low pay and poverty are national problems. But they are of a different magnitude and significance in the North. In the North unemployment is endemic; it is long-term; it robs people of any future. In the South, unemployment is lower; it is less likely to be long term; there is still some hope.

There has been a sharp increase in the proportion of the male workforce as a whole receiving low wages (for women, it is little changed at a much worse level)–in the North, for example, the proportion has doubled. This evidence is quite contradictory to the government's argument of people pricing themselves out of jobs.

The government report to the European Commission shows that they do not expect regional differences to diminish by the end of the decade. But that is not because the process generating increasing regional inequalities is unstoppable. It is simply that the government has abandoned regional policy. Without it, economic and social division will be a permanent feature of a so-called United Kingdom.

CHAPTER 6

Impoverishing women

Caroline Glendinning

Women, of all ages, have borne much of the brunt of the increasing poverty and social inequality of the last eight years. In the first place, women have experienced attacks on their incomes and standards of living, whether these are derived from paid work or from state or private systems of welfare. Secondly, they have witnessed a steady erosion of their rights to work and at work, and their entitlement to an independent income when out of work. Thirdly, the quality of women's lives has been yet further reduced because economic and social policies have increased the amount of *unpaid* work which women are expected to perform in the home and family. This chapter describes how women have been particularly vulnerable to the effects of Thatcherite policies in the labour market and income maintenance systems. It then discusses the consequences of these policies for the work and responsibilities which women bear within the home and family.

Demographic changes

Not all of the increase in women's poverty during the last eight years can be directly attributed to government policies. Over that time the two groups of women who are at greatest risk of poverty have increased in size as a result of longer term demographic trends. First, the numbers of elderly and very elderly people have continued to grow. In all age cohorts there are far more elderly women than men, a difference which increases among the very elderly (80 +); because of differential marriage and mortality rates, elderly women of all ages are less likely to be married than their male counterparts;[1] and in all age cohorts, non-married elderly women are more likely to have lower incomes than elderly lone men or married couples, or are more likely to be dependent on supplementary benefit (SB).[2] The past eight years have therefore seen increasing numbers of elderly women experiencing an impoverished old age.

Secondly, separation and divorce have continued to cause an increase in the numbers of lone parents, from 849,000 in 1979 to 950,000 in 1983. Almost all lone parents are women and, like elderly women, lone mothers have a very high – and increasing – risk of poverty. In 1979 50.6 per cent of lone parent families lived on SB or had incomes below 140 per cent of SB

50

rates; by 1983 this had increased to 60 per cent.[3]

While these increases in the numbers of elderly women and lone mothers are not direct consequences of government policies, there has apparently been no official acknowledgement of the implications of these demographic trends for women, nor any attempt to mitigate their impact on women's experience of poverty. Indeed, the reverse is true, for the policies of the last eight years have actually increased the risk of poverty among current and future generations of elderly women and lone mothers, among others.

Employment, poverty and insecurity

Conservative economic and employment policies have hit women in paid work in three ways: first, by increasing women's vulnerability to redundancy and unemployment; secondly, by encouraging a restructuring of the labour market which has adversely affected the types of jobs and levels of pay women can obtain; and thirdly, by eroding their statutory rights when in work.

Unemployment

Women who have paid jobs are concentrated disproportionately in the public sector. They comprise 41 per cent of the total labour force, but 47 per cent of public sector employees (including 78 per cent of NHS and 86 per cent of local authority health and personal social services employees). This concentration makes women's jobs immediately and directly vulnerable to cuts in public spending. In addition, the number of employees in private sector service industries, in which women are also concentrated, fell slightly between 1979 and 1983.[4]

Overall, between 1979 and 1986 male unemployment rose by 143 per cent, from 887,200 to 2,159,600; during the same period female unemployment rose by 189 per cent, from 346,700 to 1,001,700.[5] Until 1983 both male and female unemployment grew rapidly; since then male unemployment has levelled off and fallen slightly, but unemployment has continued to rise among women. The continued rise in women's unemployment has, ironically, happened in spite of the fact that the November 1982 change in the method of calculating unemployment figures actually increased the invisibility of women's unemployment. The former basis (Jobcentre registrations) certainly undercounted the numbers of unemployed women – after the switch to counting actual benefit claimants, 14 per cent of women were immediately removed from the unemployment figures (but only 5 per cent of men).[6]

Women have also been disproportionately excluded from the government's special employment measures. From October 1984 access was restricted to those 'in receipt of benefit' – narrowly interpreted as those actually making claims for unemployment benefit or SB. Many married women are, of course, not in this position. In particular, their access to jobs

51

on the Community Programme was affected – it was estimated that 33 per cent of female but only 10 per cent of male CP participants would be affected by the changes.[7] The same restriction will also affect women's access to the new Job Training scheme, penalising especially married women wishing to retrain on TOPS and 'mature returners' courses after a period out of the labour market.

Part-time work and low pay

Women may not have experienced widespread full-time unemployment to quite the same extent as men, but they have nevertheless experienced increasing restrictions on the types of jobs available to them and an associated decline in pay and working conditions. While the number of women in full-time employment has continued to decline since 1981, the number of part-time jobs has risen – between 1981 and 1985 by around 700,000 – almost all of these jobs being performed by women. Moreover, the average number of hours worked by part-time women workers has fallen, especially among manual employees.[8]

To some extent these changes reflect employers' responses to the economic recession through increasing productivity and workforce flexibility, but they have also been encouraged by government subsidies through the MSC job-splitting scheme.

Part-time work invariably means lower hourly rates of pay. Moreover, during the last ten years the hourly earnings of women in part-time employment have actually declined relative to the hourly earnings of both women and men employed full-time in the same occupations and industries.[9] Increasing numbers of part-time workers now earn weekly wages below the threshold at which they become liable for national insurance contributions (£38.00 in 1986/7). The number earning below this lower limit increased by 0.5 million since 1979, to 2.75 million in 1984. Altogether, some 60 per cent of part-time employees currently earn below the limit, and their numbers are increasing.[10]

Not paying national insurance contributions not only keeps down employers' wages bills; it also disqualifies increasing numbers of women workers from statutory sick pay, unemployment and invalidity benefits, maternity pay and, in the future, retirement pensions. (Most part-time workers are also ineligible for occupational benefits in sickness, maternity and old age.) Shorter hours and increasing use of short-term contracts also mean other losses – paid meal breaks and paid holidays, for example.

Far from trying to halt the relative decline in the pay of part-time women workers, government actions to deregulate the labour market have had a disproportionate effect on women's pay. The Wages Act 1986 removed wages council minimum wage protection from workers aged under 21 and weakened protection for adults. Three-quarters of wages council workers are women – two-thirds of them work part-time. The Wages Act also weakened rights to challenge unfair deductions from wages – an increasing

52

problem in the retail sector where 63 per cent of the workforce are women. Finally, the move towards privatisation of public sector services that has flowed from the removal of the Fair Wages Resolution has largely hit women workers in sectors such as cleaning, catering and laundries.

Losing rights at work
While part-time work may enable women to combine employment and domestic responsibilities, their rights in such jobs have been systematically under attack. Women who work less than 16 hours a week (or if they work 8 but less than 16 hours a week and have less than five years' continuous service with the same employer) have no rights under the 1975 Employment Protection Act to protection against unfair dismissal, to redundancy pay or to reinstatement after maternity leave. About two-thirds of part-time local authority manual employees, for example, currently work less than 16 hours per week and are therefore likely to have no such protection.[11] Significantly, the MSC job-splitting scheme lent official sanction to this lack of protection by only subsidising jobs of up to 15 hours a week. It is likely that the new Job Share scheme, launched on 6 April 1987 to supersede the job-splitting scheme, will require employers to create part-time jobs of at least 15 hours per week. But this minimum may, many critics argue, become a maximum.

Even women who work for more than the 16-hour weekly threshold have been hit. In 1979 the qualifying period for protection against unfair dismissal was increased from 26 to 52 weeks. The 1980 Employment Act increased it further, to two years, for small businesses with up to 20 employees (exactly the kinds of firms in which women workers are concentrated), and in 1985 the two-year qualifying period was extended to all employees. The 1980 Act also extended to two years the period for which a woman has to work before being entitled to reinstatement after maternity leave; made more complex the administrative procedures she must comply with in order to return; and exempted firms with fewer than six employees from any duty to reinstate *or* offer alternative employment to a woman after maternity leave if this is not 'reasonably practicable'.

Women's rights would be eroded even further under proposals in the 1986 White Paper *Building businesses . . . not barriers*. These include raising the hours of work threshold from 16 to 20 per week to qualify for major employment rights after two years, and from eight to 12 hours to qualify after five years; and exempting firms with fewer than 10 employees from the obligation to allow a woman to return to work after maternity leave. Raising the hours of work threshold would immediately disqualify 294,000 part-time workers – 95 per cent of whom are women – from all main employment rights; and, together with the exemption of small firms, will mean 'that the majority of pregnant working women will not qualify for a statutory right to reinstatement.'[12]

The only actions which have been taken to promote women's rights at work have been forced upon a reluctant British government by the EEC. To comply with the 1975 EEC Equal Pay Directive, a European Court of Justice decision of July 1982 forced the government to extend the Equal Pay Act from January 1984 to cover work of 'equal value'. This extension could enable inequalities in pay to be challenged in the many situations where job segregation had previously made direct comparisons impossible. Similar infringement proceedings by the European Commission against the government's implementation of the 1976 EEC Equal Treatment Directive led to the extension of the Equal Pay Act in 1986 to cover employers with fewer than five employees. Nevertheless, it is difficult to anticipate what impact these amendments will actually have on women's pay. Although the history of both Acts suggests that their effects have been minimal,[13] the 'equal value' amendment may provide a means of tackling some of the structural inequalities in the labour market which lower women's pay.

Poverty and welfare

Women's disadvantage in the labour market also affects their access to social security benefits and the levels of the benefits they do receive. These disadvantages have increased enormously; women are less likely than men, now and in the future, to be entitled to benefits at all, and are more likely to receive lower levels of benefits, than in 1979.

Privatising welfare
One of the main thrusts of welfare policy since 1979 has been the privatisation of social security provision. This was the initial motivation behind the 1983 review of pensions and it characterised the transfer to employers of responsibility for sick pay in 1983 and maternity benefits in 1987. Private and occupational welfare provision, whilst not directly discriminatory, does nevertheless disadvantage women indirectly in a number of ways. Such schemes are usually designed with typically male non-manual employment patterns in mind – full-time, unbroken employment with earnings peaking in the last years before retirement. Women's working patterns mean that they have difficulty fulfilling these conditions, if indeed they are eligible at all. For example, two-thirds of occupational pension schemes in one survey excluded part-time workers altogether and in a further 15 per cent participants had to work a minimum number of hours a week (usually between 16 and 24) in order to join.[14]

Similarly, occupational sick pay cover is low for part-time women workers;[15] and large groups of women (especially doing unskilled or semi-skilled work in small private sector firms) receive no occupational maternity pay.[16]

Under the statutory sick pay (SSP) scheme, paid through employers rather than the state, women are again less likely to be eligible than men. While part-time workers are in principle eligible for SSP, it has not been

54

extended to cover those earning below the national insurance contribution threshold. There is evidence of some employers 'opting out' of or refusing to pay SSP; putting pressure on employees to become self-employed or unemployed; or simply dismissing them, in order to avoid liability for SSP.[17] Similar problems are expected with the introduction of statutory maternity pay (SMP) in April 1987:

> Women employees are already often in the sort of low paid part-time jobs where problems with SSP have been experienced. In the future, it seems that these women will be at risk of increased insecurity and exploitation from employers if they become pregnant.[18]

Many women currently eligible for the maternity allowance will not qualify for SMP (see below), and many of those who do qualify will lose out because the new benefit is subject to tax and national insurance payments.

Restricted access to benefits
During the past eight years a number of national insurance social security benefits have either become more difficult to obtain or have been abolished altogether. Again, although these changes have in principle been gender-neutral, in practice they have had a far more damaging impact on women than men. Perhaps the clearest example of this effective indirect discrimination is in the new regulations governing claimants' 'availability for work' as a condition of eligibility for unemployment benefit. Since 1982 claimants have been asked whether they would take any full-time job they could do and, if there was any doubt, what arrangements had been made for the care of dependants.[19] A yet further strengthened test, introduced in the latter half of 1986, requires all new claimants to be prepared to take *any* full-time job immediately, work beyond the normal travelling distance, and make immediate arrangements for family care – requirements which will clearly penalise women claimants seeking part-time work or with family responsibilities far more than men.

Secondly, as well as being low paid, women are also far more likely than men to have their work interrupted by periods at home caring for children or other dependants, during which they pay no national insurance contributions. They have, therefore, been disproportionately hit by the abolition in 1986 of reduced rate national insurance benefits for unemployed and other claimants with only partial contribution records. In 1985 21,838 – the vast majority of whom would have had no independent entitlement to any other source of income – received reduced benefits.[20] Thirdly, women's typically low pay and discontinuous employment patterns have restricted the access of around 94,000 women[21] to income during maternity, especially for second and subsequent pregnancies, because entitlement to statutory maternity pay since April 1987 has been dependent on a recent history of national insurance contributions and continuous employment with the same employer. (The number of women expected to gain from this change is only 20,000.)

It is important to remember that for women who are married or cohabiting (as were 68 per cent of working age women in the 1981 census), the loss of these national insurance benefits means the loss of entitlement to *any* independent income of their own while not earning, because their partner's resources will generally preclude claims for means-tested benefits. The erosion of the national insurance scheme is, therefore, of particular significance for women.

Directed equal treatment

As with employment, the only measures which have been taken over the past eight years to improve women's access to social security benefits have been forced on the government by an EEC directive. But, again, the implementation of this has been grudging and far from effective. Regulations introduced in 1983, which in principle allowed claims for means-tested SB and family income supplement (FIS) to be made by either the man or woman in a couple, in fact restricted claims to those who had recent (within the last six months) contact with the labour market, thus excluding women who were likely to have had longer periods at home caring. Moreover, the majority of women who have claimed benefits under these regulations have been unsuccessful; in 1984 only 30 per cent of FIS claims and 40 per cent of SB claims from married women were successful.[22] One of the very few advances for women in the Social Security Act 1986 is the removal of these restrictions on a couple's choice as to who should be the claimant.

The main advantage which women have gained from the EEC Social Security Equal Treatment Directive has been the extension of invalid care allowance to some 50,000 married and cohabiting women carers who have no other source of independent income. Yet this was only achieved 18 months *after* the implementation of the Directive, and then only in the face of a humiliating government defeat in the European Court.

Declining value of benefits

As well as finding their access to benefits restricted, women have experienced cuts in the value of some of the benefits they do receive – and these cuts are likely to continue in the future. Most importantly, child benefit – for many women the only money over which they have complete control, and essential in meeting their children's needs[23] – was cut in value in 1980 and 1985. The 1980 cut was made good in the 1983 election year. The 1985 cut has not been reversed – leaving child benefit worth 29p less than in 1983 and 3 per cent less than in April 1979.

Women also stand to lose considerably from the measures in the 1986 Social Security Act, both in the immediate and the longer term future. The almost complete invisibility of women in both the Green and White Papers which preceded this legislation was remarkable, despite the growing numbers of women facing poverty in old age, as single parents and as low paid workers.

- *Income support*: almost half of all lone mothers currently receive SB. Some 150,000 of these long-term claimants will be worse off because of the loss of the higher long-term scale rate and additional requirements (extra weekly payments).[24] By ignoring the impact of work expenses on their net earnings, the calculation of earnings disregards will penalise women who pay for child care to enable them to take up paid employment.

- *Family credit*: one of the few victories against the government's proposals was the retention of family credit (which will replace FIS) as a cash benefit payable to women, rather than as a (male) wage supplement. Nevertheless, take-up of family credit is expected to be low (60 per cent); much of its increased value will be cancelled out by cuts in housing benefit and the loss of free school meals; and the need to reapply every six months or with each job change will increase the financial pressures on hard-pressed women with children. Official figures also show that the poorest working lone parents will be worse off despite the extra resources going into family credit.

- *Free school meals*: 545,000 children whose parents currently claim FIS or who are on a very low income will lose their entitlement to free school meals. The increase in family credit equivalent to 60p per school day will be too low to buy a secondary school meal in over half the local education authorities in the country; other families on low incomes will receive no compensation at all.[25] Again, it is women who will be responsible for making ends meet on a reduced income; who will suffer yet more job losses and cuts in hours in the school meal service; and who will have additional unpaid work at home instead making packed lunches for their children.

- *Social fund*: the replacement of SB single payments by loans recoverable from future benefit will place enormous pressures on women already having difficulty budgeting on an inadequate weekly income.

- *Maternity grant*: women who do not receive SB (income support) or FIS (family credit) including mothers under 16 years old, have lost the universal £25 maternity grant. Social fund maternity grant of £80 for those who are on these benefits is less than half the current maximum SB single payment entitlement for maternity needs.

- *Widows*: many, especially those without children, will lose from changes to widow's benefits.

- *Women with disabilities*: given the preponderance of women in the elderly population and the association between old age and disability, many more women than men will be hit by the loss of the long-term rate of SB and needs-related additional requirements for elderly people and those with disabilities. The new disability and pensioner premiums will not fully compensate for these.[26]

- *Carers of elderly and disabled people*: again overwhelmingly women, carers are the *only* group who will lose the higher long-term rate of SB and not receive a 'client group' premium in compensation.

● *SERPS*: women who retire after the year 2000 will find that the switch from the 'best 20 years' to lifetime earnings as the basis for calculating pension levels and the reduction of SERPS from 25 to 20 per cent of earnings will cut the earnings related component of their pensions by about half.[27] The alternative protection to the 'best 20 years' rule proposed for women with children will penalise those women who take part-time work earning more than the national insurance threshold, while giving some protection to those who stay at home to care for their children full time. Women earning below the national insurance threshold will still not be entitled to an adequate pension. In the future, even more elderly women will have to rely on means-tested benefits in old age.

Independence in taxation

One sphere in which the government has held itself out as recognising the independent role of women is that of taxation. The first stated objective of the Green Paper on the Reform of Personal Taxation, published on Budget day 1986, was 'to give married women the same opportunity for privacy and independence in tax matters as their husbands'. But as CPAG argued in its response, 'with regard to both privacy and independence, the Green Paper is selling an essentially false prospectus that fails to meet the growing demands for the elimination of sex discrimination in the tax system which provided the original impetus for reform'.[28]

The proposed system of transferable allowances (under which any unused tax allowance could be transferred to an employed spouse) would not guarantee women privacy in their tax affairs; nor would it be compatible with genuine independent taxation. Worse still, independent analysis confirmed many people's fears that such a system would act as a serious disincentive to married women to return to paid employment.

As the *Daily Telegraph*'s economics correspondent warned, 'the important issue is that Lawson's reforms will harm ordinary working women, the vast majority of whom work part-time for low wages. Some suspect a plot to force women to stay at home and thus relieve the dole queues.'[29] The financial secretary tried to dismiss such fears with the observation: 'I have not yet encountered a complaint from a husband that his wife will not let him go back to work because she is worried about her own tax bill increasing.'[30] It is remarks such as these which serve to demonstrate ministers' lack of understanding of the power imbalance between men and women and the continued hold of traditional ideas about sex roles.

Indeed, the system of transferable allowances would serve to reinforce such ideas. The Green Paper made clear that 'the Government believe that the tax system should not discriminate against families where the wife wishes to remain at home to care for young children. Transferable allowances would direct more tax relief to such families' (para 3.18). The proposal was based on a very traditional model of the family in which the mother should stay at home to care for young children. Extra support for such families is then channelled to the wage-earning male in the form of extra tax relief, rather than to the woman at home in the form of a cash benefit. Fears about the implications of transferable allowances for women, in particular, together with concern at the wastefulness of such a strategy, have led to considerable opposition to the government's proposals. As noted in chapter 15, the government is therefore having second thoughts. However, it seems unlikely, from everything ministers have said so far, that this will lead to proposals for a genuinely independent system of taxation.

Increasing women's unpaid work

Women have been especially vulnerable to Conservative public spending policies, not only because of their concentration in public sector employment but also because many of the services provided by the public sector help to relieve the burden of *unpaid* caring and domestic work which women undertake in the home. The corollary of this is, of course, that cuts in spending and levels of public services shift responsibility back to the unpaid, domestic sphere. This shift has been buttressed by forceful ideological statements about the role of the home and family: 'it really all starts in the family, because the family [is] the most important means through which we show our care for others'.[31] Nowhere have statements such as this one by Margaret Thatcher been made more explicitly than in relation to policies of 'community care' for elderly and disabled people. So:

> ... the primary sources of support and care for elderly people are informal and voluntary. These spring from the personal ties of kinship, friendship and neighbourhood ... It is the role of public authorities to sustain and, where necessary, develop – but never to displace – such support and care. Care *in* the community must increasingly mean care *by* the community.[32]

In a number of direct and indirect ways, government policies have withdrawn support from women in their capacity as carers. So far as childcare is concerned, statutory duties to provide pre-school education were removed from local authorities by the 1980 Education Act. Pressures on local spending have squeezed what nursery and pre-school provision remains; one of the earliest casualties, for example, was the entire range of nursery school services in Oxfordshire. The 1980 Education Act removed the duty to provide school meals other than to those entitled to free meals (to which entitlement was also cut back) and allowed local education authorities to change what they wished, while at the same time abolishing nutritional standards. This led to a big drop in demand for school meals, with the proportion of children taking school meals falling from 64 per cent in 1979 to 49 per cent in 1986, thereby shifting responsibility for children's day-time nutrition back on to the family.[33] A further element of support for working mothers was withdrawn in 1985 by the enforcement of tax liability on workplace nursery provision. Cuts in state provision for childcare have been paralleled by a corresponding increase in informal and voluntary arrangements – childminding, playgroups and privately employed 'nannies' – all of which involve women in typically low paid or unpaid 'voluntary' work in a largely unregulated and unprotected private service sector.

At the other end of the life cycle, public spending on health and personal social services has failed to keep pace with the increasing numbers of disabled and frail elderly people. In the absence of help from statutory services, the pressure on female relatives and neighbours to provide essential help to elderly people will only increase.

Bearing the burden of poverty

Less directly, women bear the burden of managing poverty on a day-to-day basis. Whether they live alone or with a partner, on benefits or low earnings, it is usually women who are responsible for making ends meet and for managing the debts which result when they don't. Indeed, the lower the household income, the more likely it is that this responsibility will rest with women. As more women and men lose their jobs, and as benefits are cut or decline in value, women are increasingly caught in a daily struggle to feed and clothe their families – usually only at considerable personal sacrifice:

'When the children are in bed, I turn the heating off and use a blanket or an extra cardigan' (lone mother on SB).

'You do get a lot of tension trying to make ends meet . . . And the worst part of being unemployed is having always to be broke . . . thinking over where's the next money going to come from' (unemployed married woman).[34]

While the history books will record Mrs Thatcher's major achievement in becoming Britain's first woman prime minister, testimonies such as these demonstrate that, ironically, it is women who have had to bear the brunt of the increased poverty over which she has presided.

Many thanks to Karen Clarke, Claire Callendar and Susan Lonsdale for their invaluable help in compiling this chapter.

60

CHAPTER 7

Second-class citizens

Hilary Arnott

To look at the black experience in Britain since 1979 is to expose the effects
of Conservative policies at their harshest, with few if any palliative gestures
to hide the stark reality of life for deprived minorities in the 1980s. Black*
people came to this country as units of labour (their dependants were made
unwelcome, considered unnecessary appendages) and have continued to be
regarded as such. So, over a period of massive industrial change, they have
in turn been recruited, exploited *and* discarded at will.

Origins of discrimination and racism

Unemployment and low pay are not new to black people in Britain. They, or
their parents or grandparents, came to this country in the 1950s and 1960s
not just because they were encouraged to do so – because then there were too
few workers, not too few jobs – but also because the economies in their home
countries had been underdeveloped and perverted by colonialism and could
no longer provide them with a livelihood. So, in response to direct recruit-
ment drives and economic pressure, people from the Caribbean, India and
Pakistan came to fill the dirty, unskilled jobs – characterised by low pay, bad
conditions and unsocial hours – that local white workers did not want and
could, at that time, choose not to do.

Initially, their social needs (housing, health, welfare) were ignored –
'migrant' workers are regarded as labour units and are not meant to have
families. So these new black workers were left to fend for themselves, mainly in the already overcrowded inner-city areas of the large conurbations,
competing with the indigenous white population for already inadequate
resources. In turn, the black workers, rather than the inadequate resources,
were blamed for causing social problems. The ideology of racism was there
to be exploited.

So, by 1962, as the post-war employment boom began to subside, the

---

* By black we mean all non-white groups whose common experience of racial oppression
outweighs socio-cultural difference. It is how Afro-Caribbeans and Asians, particularly the
young, choose to describe themselves.

immigration of black labour was restricted by an Act that enshrined racism in immigration law and on the statute book – in other words, institutionalised it. Having made black people second-class citizens, that institutional racism could then be brought to bear in other areas – for example, in housing, with discriminatory public housing policies, and in education, with quotas and bussing. Successive restrictions on black immigration followed until, with the 1971 Immigration Act all, 'primary' black immigration was effectively halted. But this did not stop the immigration issue from being used to exploit racialism. Margaret Thatcher, in the run-up to the local elections (one year before the 1979 general election), undercut the extreme right-wing parties by assuring the nation that the Conservatives would 'finally see an end to immigration' as 'this country might be rather swamped by people with a different culture'.

With these words she set the climate for her governments. The 1979 Conservative manifesto, although promoting the idea of equal rights for all those 'legally' settled here, promised even more restrictions on the entry of dependants (what price family policy?) – and all this under a section headed 'The rule of law'! In this atmosphere, and with the further pledge to dismantle sections of the Race Relations Act and curtail the powers of the Commission for Racial Equality – the very limited state machinery committed to tackling discrimination – it is little wonder that the Conservative government held out no promise for black people.

The facts of racial disadvantage

→ *Unemployment*
Unemployment has devastated sections of the working population of this country. But the black population has been hit by far the hardest.[1] This division began well before 1979. By 1979 the unemployment rate for white women was 5.7 per cent, while for black women it was 10.8 per cent; and while 4.4 per cent of white men were unemployed, the figure for black men was 6 per cent. These average figures masked startlingly high rates for young black people.

By the spring of 1985 the unemployment rate for black men had more than trebled and was almost twice that for white men – 20 per cent and 11 per cent respectively. Among black women it was 19 per cent, compared with 10 per cent for white women, and for black 16-24-year-olds it was 33 per cent, compared with 16 per cent for young white people.

As if these figures were not bad enough, for certain sections within the black community the picture was even bleaker. The Pakistani and Bangladeshi communities have been particularly adversely affected – 48 per cent of economically active 16-24-year-olds were unemployed in 1985, as were 44 per cent (of all working ages) and 35 per cent of men aged 45 to 64.

People living in certain areas, especially those in the inner cities, are also hit harder than the average. For example a local survey in Liverpool in 1986 stated that black unemployment had reached a staggering 80 per cent; while back in 1983 a study by Leicester City Council found that 55 per cent of Afro-Caribbean and 54 per cent of Asians aged 60 to 64 were unemployed, compared with 20 per cent of white people of the same age. This same survey revealed that although the figure for white unemployed 16-19-year-olds was high – at 24 per cent – for Afro-Caribbeans of the same age, it was 46 per cent. At the same time a Bradford Council survey found that figures for black youth unemployment were artificially *depressed*, both by the fact that more black young people stay on in education and by their high involvement in youth training schemes.

To cap it all, black people are likely to remain unemployed for longer than white people. A national survey by the Policy Studies Institute (PSI) in 1983 found that half of all black unemployed men had been registered as unemployed for more than a year, compared to a third of white men.[2] A local survey in Preston, in 1984, found that 73.2 per cent of the black unemployed had been without work for three years or more.[3]

Training schemes
Many young black people have turned to the various MSC training schemes as a way out of the unemployment trap. But, so far, all the evidence points to the fact that the Youth Training Scheme and other similar schemes are simply reproducing the discrimination to be found in the labour market. So, in 1984 in London, only 45 per cent of Afro-Caribbean trainees were on 'Mode A' (ie, employer-based) schemes, with their better long-term employment prospects, compared with 70 per cent of white trainees.[4] While in central Manchester the following year, out of a total 279 schemes, 100 of the employer schemes had no ethnic minority trainees at all and 44 per cent of black trainees were located in just six schemes.[5] A recent report from the National Youth Bureau accuses YTS of perpetuating rather than overcoming the inequalities: 'Racism and discrimination . . . became manifest throughout the process.'[6]

Low pay
Black people who do have a job are, on average, paid much less than white people. They are concentrated in the low wage sectors of employment. For example, black men are almost four times as likely as white men to be working in the hotel and catering industry,[7] a sector notorious for its low wages and poor working conditions, and one where the demise of wages council protection for young people may lead to wages being cut even further. The figures for black and white women in the hotel and catering industry are identical, reflecting the low status work that many women, whatever their colour, are subjected to.

The lack of ordinary employment opportunities, particularly for Asian women, is reflected in the growth of self-employment. However, in this

63

case, self-employment is a euphemism for homeworking, with its extremely low pay, long hours and lack of employment rights. Thus the 1984 PSI study found that the proportion of Asian women workers who were self-employed was double that for white women (14 per cent and 7 per cent).

There are no recent figures available on the pay that black people actually take-home. But in 1982 there were considerable discrepancies between the median weekly earnings of white male workers and those of Afro-Caribbeans and Asians–£129.00, compared with £109.20 and £110.70–and for Bangladeshi men the figure fell to £88.00.[8] Bangladeshi women's average weekly take-home pay was a mere £43.80, almost half that of Afro-Caribbean women. The latter, at £81.20, actually did better than white women (£77.50). But these 'higher' earnings were achieved at a cost: Afro-Caribbean women are more likely to be doing shift work, especially at night, and they tend to have a longer working day than white women.

Discrimination in the labour market
All this evidence reinforces the numerous surveys that have proved, again and again, that black people continue to be discriminated against in the labour market. In fact, the PSI report found that the situation had not improved at all compared with ten years earlier.[9] Yet a recent House of Commons select committee report, while commenting on the 'substantial' level of racial discrimination in employment, made no recommendations on action that private employers could take to combat this.[10] Nor did it recommend the practice of 'contract compliance', whereby private companies must fulfil certain non-discriminatory practices when supplying a public body.

Jobless, or in low paid employment, the majority of black people have also been trapped in the inner cities–Britain's Bantustans. In the 1960s and 1970s, these metropolitan areas were fighting against advancing poverty and decay. In the 1980s, with Conservative cuts in rate support grant and rate capping, any chances of combating urban decay have been destroyed. In Birmingham, for example, the government has reduced the rate support grant from £295m in 1978/9 to £180m in 1985/6–and most of the rate-capped authorities contain significant black populations.[11]

Immigration and the welfare state

Caught in this cycle of poverty, most black people, like anyone else living in Britain, are fully entitled to claim state benefits. They should, in theory, experience no more difficulties than anyone else. But as A. Sivanandan so succinctly put it, 'it was their labour that was wanted, not their presence'.[12] And as early as 1948, when the Beveridge plan was being put into effect, a colonial office official warned that 'the Mother Country social services will attract more and more of these [black] people as time goes on'.[13] This view, that black people would try and enter the country and then 'scrounge' off the system, has continued to be exploited ever since and immigration status has been inextricably linked to benefit entitlement. In particular, with the 1971 Immigration Act, increasing numbers of people have been allowed entry only on condition that they have 'no recourse to public funds'.

No recourse to public funds
However, it was not until the 1980 Social Security Act and its regulations that specific classes of immigrants were excluded by law from receiving benefits. The effect of this has been wide reaching.

First, there are those directly excluded – and this does not just mean visitors, but also those who plan to settle here. For example, fiancés of British citizens (if they are lucky enough to evade the 'primary purpose' rule in the first place) are not eligible for benefits. Yet neither can they work until the Home Office restrictions are lifted – a Catch-22 situation which in some cases can take months to be resolved, and then sometimes only with the intervention of MPs and advice agencies. Then there are those cases where the rules are misapplied and people who have every right to benefits are denied them.

There are also those who, through no fault of their own, get caught in the web woven by the Home Office in conjunction with the DHSS. Take the case of Parveen Khan who came to the UK and married Shankat Khan in 1979. It transpired that technically Shankat, who had entered the country at the age of 13, was an illegal immigrant. In November 1981 the couple, who by then had two children, were told that as illegal immigrants they were both to be removed. From March 1982 until August of the following year, while the appeals were going through, Parveen's supplementary benefit and child benefit (her children were born in this country) were withdrawn. The Home Office then stated she was not, after all, an illegal immigrant.

The Home Office maintained in this case that it was not responsible for the DHSS refusal of benefit. But the DHSS, clearly acting in this sort of case as an arm of immigration control, accepted the Home Office's view of Parveen Khan's situation and deprived her and her children of their rights. Had it not been for the support raised by the campaign mounted around her case they would literally have been starved out of the country.

Passport-checking
An important consequence of the link between immigration status and entitlement to benefit is the discriminatory practice of checking people's passports. Although the *S Manual* now tells DHSS staff to 'make every effort to deal with cases without asking to see passports' – the *Manual* was modified in 1982 after complaints about the use of passport checking – the practice of DHSS staff asking to see the passports of black claimants still appears to be widespread. A year after the revised guidance a survey in Oldham found that only 18 out of 77 DHSS officers did *not* check passports. Anyone who is black, particularly if they look Asian or do not speak fluent

English, are often assumed to have 'recently come from abroad' and therefore are asked for their passports. A Tameside man who came to this country as 'recently' as 1938 was asked for his!

Besides the implicit assumption that behind every black face there is a 'scrounger', passport checks run the risk that DHSS staff, who are not, after all, employed as immigration officers, will misinterpret the stamps in the passport or the rules about eligibility and as a result wrongfully deny benefits.

Passport-checking also occurs in the fields of housing, education and health. The latter was exacerbated first by the October 1979 DHSS circular 'Gatecrashers', which advised London health authorities of their role in ensuring eligibility for free treatment; and secondly, by the introduction four years later of National Health Service charges for certain categories of people coming from abroad. These charges were introduced, following orchestrated claims in parliament and the media about scroungers, despite the fact that a 1981 DHSS pilot survey of abuse – the only empirical study of its kind – showed no evidence to support such allegations. However, the effects were immediate in terms of increasing passport checks. After the 1979 Circular, for example, there were numerous reported cases of checks by hospital officials, including one on a member of the Commission for Racial Equality who had been settled here for 14 years and another on a Pakistani doctor practising in Nottingham.

Racist attitudes and take-up
The prevalence of passport-checking is linked to the racist attitude displayed by some DHSS officers, as evidenced in the PSI's tempered observations: 'Since racial prejudice is so widespread in society, it is not surprising that it should be found among local office staff.'[15] All this cannot inspire black people with the confidence that they will be treated correctly and given their rightful entitlement. That is, if they are prepared to overcome the stigma and ask for their rights in the first place. A 1984 survey in Islington showed that potential Bengali and Greek Cypriot claimants feared that to claim would cause 'trouble', and so did not take-up their entitlement to benefits.[16]

Take-up among black people is also adversely affected by other barriers such as language. In 1980 the DHSS was still maintaining that 'it was difficult to determine whether problems of communication represent a serious obstacle to ethnic minority claimants'. In response, the Parliamentary Home Affairs Committee severely criticised it for its lack of interest in or initiative to overcome the problems of black claimants. Few visible efforts to improve access and take-up have been made since then, beyond the translation of the leaflet 'Which Benefit' into six languages and the production of a multi-lingual poster.

Fowler's reviews
Norman Fowler's social security reviews, proclaimed as 'the most substantial examination of the . . . system since the Beveridge report', did not address any of these problems. Rather, they recommended the extension of the 'presence test' for benefits to prevent 'too ready access to help by those who have no recent links with this country.' (Some benefits are already subject to 'presence' tests, eg, child benefit – six months, severe disablement allowance – 10 years.) In the event, the proposal was dropped – one of the successes of the campaigners against the Green Paper plans. But the intention was clear: more black people were to be excluded or discouraged from claiming benefits and, again, the knock-on effect on black people settled here would have been even more checks and even greater poverty.

Other aspects of the Social Security Act 1986 – the end product of the reviews – though not overtly aimed at black people, must adversely affect their position. The introduction of a lower rate of benefit for single childless under-25-year-olds on income support will fall particularly hard on black families, where not only is the youth unemployment rate so high, but the parents too are more likely to be unemployed or low paid. The cutbacks in SERPs will weaken the position of those who have not spent the whole of their working life in this country. Moreover, how will black people fare under the discretionary social fund where there will be more scope for, but no right of appeal against, racist decisions or mistaken assumptions – for example, that Asian women can always turn to the extended family for support? More generally, the shift to a greater emphasis on means-tested provision has disturbing implications because it is means-tested benefits that count as 'public funds' under the recourse to public funds rule.

Sponsorship
This definition of public funds was contained in the 1985 amended Immigration Rules – which specified the main means-tested benefits (supplementary benefit, family income supplement and housing benefit). In turn, the term 'no recourse to public funds' was linked to one particular aspect of the immigration/welfare benefits connection – that of sponsorship – which merits special attention as it clearly illustrates how certain categories of black people are *never* to be considered equal.

The notion of sponsorship, where a sponsor is liable to maintain a relative coming from abroad 'without recourse to public funds', was also introduced in the 1971 Act. But since November 1980 it has been linked to the supplementary benefit regulations, so that any arrangement made after 23 May 1983 means that there is a legally enforceable liability to maintain a sponsored person and failure to do so could mean prosecution.

In practice, prosecution might be unlikely, but the insecurity engendered is real enough. In addition, although the fact that a person has been sponsored 'does not of itself affect title to benefit'; in practice, claimants who have been told, incorrectly, that they are ineligible, not surprisingly, have often withdrawn their claims. Others have not even dared claim in the first place for fear that this might affect their immigration status – for example, women fearing removal if a claim for benefit seems to indicate that their marriage has broken up.

Finally, the sponsorship provisions create a class of people who, though settled here and fully entitled to benefit, can only claim at the risk of legal action against the relative who sponsored them originally. This provision adds another element to the notion of divided families, so prevalent in the history of immigration legislation over the last 25 years and such a contradiction to the Conservative Party's avowed concern for the family and for family life.

Information-gathering

The links between the immigration authorities and the DHSS have had another consequence, this time on the collection of information on the specific situation of black people with regard to benefits and unemployment. Since 1982, when the government announced that in future it would be collecting unemployment statistics at unemployment benefit offices on the basis of 'ethnic origin' rather than country of birth, the Department of Employment has been attempting to implement the procedure. However, an early pilot study showed a refusal rate of 33.7 per cent for self-assessment, and the DHSS unions have protested against staff assessing people visually, partly because there is no guarantee of confidentiality or against misuse of the information. To be sure, the alleged remarks of employment minister Alan Clark in early 1985 did not promote any confidence. When informed of black protest against ethnic monitoring, he was alleged to have replied: 'You mean to say that they don't want us collecting their names and addresses because they are afraid we're going to hand them over to the immigration service so that they can send them all back to Bongo Bongo land.' As *Searchlight* magazine asked:

> Is the government really intending to use the results to create job opportunities for black people? . . . On its record, the government and Mr Clark may forgive ourselves and black people from finding this just a little hard to swallow.[17]

In other aspects of living standards there are even fewer figures to show how black people are being affected by the cuts in public expenditure which have so adversely affected health, education and housing provision in the last eight years. Though, for example, after the Brixton uprisings of 1981 Lord Scarman found that there were '200-300 young blacks' in the area who were 'homeless, sleeping rough or squatting'.

Conclusion

Despite the lack of adequate statistics it is clear that many black people, and in particular black women and the 'never employed' black youth, are bearing a large part of the social impact of the government's policies: trapped by unemployment and low incomes in decaying inner-city areas where the very fabric of their surroundings is being eroded by neglect. Moreover, promises of increased aid after the 1981 riots–prior to which the Conservatives followed the free market policy of 'benign neglect'–to patch things up and inject opportunity into the inner cities, are insignificant compared with the overall scale of the cuts in rate support grant. Nor do the promises sit well with that other Conservative 'solution' to the problems of the inner cities and their tensions: coercion in the form of increasingly heavy policing.

The results of neglect and increasing discrimination were graphically and tragically seen two years ago in Broadwater Farm in North London, where 83 per cent of black youth were unemployed and 75 per cent of households had a total income of less than £8,000 a year (35 per cent less than £3,000). As the independent inquiry into the 'disturbance in October 1985' concluded: 'We do not make a simplistic link between deprivation and rioting, for the cost of unemployment and poverty can be paid in many other ways. But there is a connection: as Ernie Large (ex-Haringay councillor) said:

"If you take unemployment and poverty and top them up with oppression, you are likely to light a fuse."[19]

CHAPTER 8

Living with unemployment

David Taylor

This chapter briefly describes the collapse of employment in the early 1980s, the effects of unemployment on individuals and households, the cost of unemployment to the exchequer, and the two main features of the government's response: its attempt to define the problem away and its increasing adoption of the American 'Workfare' approach. In squeezing all this into one chapter a great deal has had to be omitted. Most importantly, women's experience of unemployment and the government's special employment measures are not discussed (but see chapter 6).

When, in 1975 Harold Wilson was savaged for allowing unemployment to rise above one million, neither he nor his critics could have imagined that only 12 years later the UK would be enduring its sixth year of unemployment above three million. And this in spite of having entered its 'seventh successive year of steady growth'.[1]

Unfortunately, as high unemployment has persisted, the initial sense of outrage among those not immediately affected has faded. Now, even informed observers seem to suspend their critical faculties when reviewing economic policies that in the early 1980s did much to create the problem, and in subsequent years have done so demonstrably little to solve it.

Large-scale unemployment is increasingly presented as regrettable but unavoidable, yet throughout the 1950s and 1960s unemployment seldom rose as high as 3 per cent, and long-term unemployment averaged less than 50,000. Although after the mid-1950s the unemployment trend was steadily rising, the 1970s' unemployment peak, reached in August 1977, was still only slightly over 1,600,000.

The real collapse of employment did not occur until 1980 and, according to a report from the all party House of Commons Treasury and Civil Service Committee, chaired by Mr Edward du Cann, the cause was not difficult to identify:

The United Kingdom is still the most open of the five large non-communist economies. This makes us particularly vulnerable to variations in external demand, whether caused by fluctuations in the exchange rate or by the world business cycle. The importance of both factors is illustrated by recent experience. Before the appreciation of sterling

70

and the world recession, in the first quarter of 1979, unemployment in the UK was 5.9 per cent. By the third quarter of 1982, it had risen to 12.9 per cent. Over the same period, unemployment in the 15 major OECD countries rose from 5.1 per cent to 8.3 per cent. Thus something under half the rise in British unemployment may plausibly be ascribed to the world recession. But why should the rise in unemployment in Britain have been so much greater than in any other comparable economy?

In answer to this question the Committee cited the evidence of Dr Emminger, the former president of the Deutsche Bundesbank, who referred to sterling's real effective exchange rate in 1980-81 in the following terms:

This is by far the most excessive overvaluation which any major currency has experienced in recent monetary history . . . The large real appreciation of sterling from 1979 to 1981 was probably the most important single element in that period's British economic policy, as concerns its effects both on domestic inflation as well as on British trade, production and unemployment.[2]

It was, of course, a government decision to maintain a particular exchange rate. The government must, therefore, accept responsibility for the economic devastation which resulted.

The unequal burden of unemployment.

Regions
The collapse of employment did not affect all industries and regions equally. Between the peak of the 1979 boom and the trough of the 1983 depression, 1,705,000 jobs were lost in manufacturing industries. The service sector suffered a net loss of 247,000 jobs. Retail distribution shed 276,000 employees, hotels and catering 84,000. 203,000 jobs were lost in the construction industry. Few sectors escaped unscathed, though banking, finance and insurance gained 122,000 new employees.

Although employment in some sectors has recovered since March 1983, it is much easier to destroy jobs than create them, and the number of new jobs has been nothing like sufficient to reduce significantly the official unemployment count. Between the 1983 trough and September 1986 manufacturing industry has lost a further 300,000 jobs, while services have gained 1,209,000.

Regionally, the South-east now has 2 per cent fewer jobs than at the time of the 1979 peak; the South-west has 2 per cent fewer; the West Midlands has 10 per cent fewer; the East Midlands has 3 per cent fewer; Yorkshire and Humberside has 12 per cent fewer; the North-west has 15 per cent fewer; the North has 13 per cent fewer. Only in East Anglia has the number of employees increased – by 9 per cent.

Unemployed people

In January 1987 the official unemployment figure stood 2¼ times higher, at 3,297,200, than in January 1979, when the figure was 1,455,300. The number of job vacancies notified to Jobcentres–at 218,100–was slightly higher in 1987 than in 1979 (214,700). In 1979 there were seven officially recorded unemployed people seeking each notified job vacancy, while in 1987 there are 15.

Even these figures present a deceptively favourable picture. There have been many changes in the coverage of the official unemployment count between 1979 and 1987, so that the 1987 figures are some half-a-million lower than they would be on the 1979 basis. In addition, the 1987 official vacancy statistics are inflated by a large number of Community Programme vacancies (30,100 in January 1987) and the recent inclusion of some 6,000 'self-employed' vacancies.

As the number of unemployed people has increased, so has the average length of time people spend out of work. Between 1979 and 1987 the average unemployment spell has risen from five months to nine months. In January 1979 334,800 people had been out of work for more than a year–24.1 per cent of all unemployed people. By January 1987 the figure had reached 1,334,400 – 40.5 per cent of the total.

Figures like these, while illustrating the recent deterioration in the labour market, can give a misleading impression that the unemployed are a static mass of people waiting for jobs. This is far from the case. Throughout 1986 an average of 407,800 people became unemployed benefit claimants each month, while an average of 406,600 people left unemployment (not necessarily the same as finding a job). It is the shifting balance between these inflows to and outflows from unemployment that determines whether the official count is rising or falling. Of the 400,000 or so people entering unemployment each month, some 66 per cent will leave the register within six months and 81 per cent within 12 months; 4 per cent will still be out of work after three years. The analogy is often drawn between the unemployed flow and the flow of a river, which graduates from a swiftly flowing surface, through slowly flowing middle depth, to the almost static deep water near the river bed, representing the very long-term unemployed, who have only a small probability of leaving unemployment.

Just as job loss and unemployment don't impinge equally on regions and industries, their impact on individuals within regions and industries is uneven. Whatever the state of the economy, younger, experienced workers, in good health and possessing the skills and qualifications required by employers, will stand the best chance of finding jobs quickly. When unemployment is high and jobs scarce, anyone with a characteristic that makes them less attractive to employers than other job-seekers risks prolonged unemployment. Such people include young inexperienced workers, older workers in their final 10 or 15 years of working life, workers with no, or few skills or qualifications, workers with a record of poor health or

72

disability and ethnic minority workers. Also, long-term unemployment can become a formidable employment obstacle in its own right. On the part of employers, anyone without a recent job reference tends to be regarded with suspicion, while on the part of unemployed workers themselves, long-term unemployment erodes work-related skills, while repeated unsuccessful job-search and rejection can undermine self-confidence and motivation.

Nearly 40 per cent of unemployed people over the age of 55 have been out of work for more than two years, compared with 25 per cent of unemployed workers between the ages of 25 and 40. This is in spite of the fact that most unemployed men aged 60 and over are taken out of the official unemployment figures by virtue of their being eligible for supplementary benefit (SB) at the long-term instead of the lower short-term rate paid to other unemployed SB claimants. The likelihood of someone between the ages of 55 and 60 leaving the unemployment count is around half that of someone aged between 20 and 30. At the other end of the age scale, in January 1987 almost 9 per cent of all unemployed benefit claimants were young people who had not held a job since leaving school.

Long-term unemployment among older workers has particularly serious repercussions. It destroys their ability to save for retirement while forcing the premature spending of any savings they might have accumulated. Indeed, SB regulations are carefully designed to ensure that all except the most modest savings are used up. As a result, large numbers of people are graduating from unemployment into retirement already in poverty, with neither savings nor investments to supplement the meagre state pension.

Unemployment among non-white ethnic minority workers is significantly higher than among white workers. The rate of unemployment among workers of West Indian origin is double that of whites, and among workers of Pakistani/Bangladeshi origin three times that of whites. Whereas white workers aged 16 to 24 have an unemployment rate of 16 per cent, the rate is 34 per cent among West Indian, and 48 per cent among Pakistani/Bangladeshi 16- to 24-year-olds. Among people over the age of 45, white workers have an unemployment rate of 7 per cent compared with a rate of 15 per cent among workers of West Indian origin and 34 per cent among workers of Pakistani/Bangladeshi origin (see also chapter 7).

Where racial prejudice among employers is concerned, it seems that the higher the qualification the greater the relative disadvantage of ethnic minority workers. So that while Pakistani/Bangladeshi men with no qualifications have an unemployment rate almost double that of their white counterparts, Pakistani/Bangladeshi men with higher qualifications have an unemployment rate more than four times that of similarly qualified white workers.

Workers with mental or physical disabilities, even though these might not present problems when they are in work, quickly find that once they are without a job, say as a result of redundancy, their disability becomes a major handicap when they have to compete with non-disabled and, in the eyes of prospective employers, more eligible job applicants. This discrimination is especially damaging to people seeking to re-integrate into society following serious illness or disability. Paid work has traditionally formed an important part of the rehabilitation process, providing a route to financial independence and social contact. The removal of employment prospects removes a ladder to normality.

People lacking marketable skills and qualifications are particularly vulnerable to unemployment, and, given the likely continued fall in demand for unskilled workers, seem likely to remain so. The 1984 Labour Force Survey shows that unemployed people with either no qualifications or CSE below grade 1 had an unemployment rate of 15.1 per cent, compared with a rate of 4.7 per cent for people with a degree or equivalent, or a teaching or nursing qualification (though even this apparently low unemployment rate represents some 170,000 people).

White, in his 1980-81 study of long-term unemployment, found that 51 per cent of men and 38 per cent of women in his sample of long-term unemployed workers were semi-skilled and unskilled manual workers. 36 per cent of women were routine non-manual workers, clerical and shop workers. In contrast, only 4 per cent of men and 5 per cent of women had worked in higher professional and administrative and lower professional and lower administrative jobs.[3]

The effects of unemployment

Poverty
The most obvious and devastating effect of unemployment – and especially long-term unemployment – is poverty, and other problems commonly associated with unemployment, such as marital breakdown, ill-health and depression, often spring from this. The 1985 Family Expenditure Survey shows that the gross income of a family whose head is unemployed for under a year was only half that of a family whose head was an employee in work. Expenditure per person in households with long-term unemployed heads, at £29.99, was 44 per cent of expenditure per person in households whose head was an employee currently employed, and 52 per cent of expenditure per head in a household with a retired head.

White notes of the long-term unemployed people in his study:

> 85 per cent were wholly or partly dependent on supplementary benefits – a system which is designed to adjust the individual's income to the minimum level required for the necessities and decencies of life. Almost half the people in our sample had been continuously unemployed for three or more years, so most of these had been living on this minimum level of financial support for at least two years. Although they did not in general come from highly paid jobs, supplementary benefit was on the average yielding something of the order of half the income which they had had from wages in their previous employment.[4]

Moylan, Miller and Davies confirm the low level of benefits to the unemployed in their report of the DHSS Cohort Study, noting that for nearly half the long-term unemployed men interviewed, total unemployment benefits received (including the now discontinued earnings related supplement) came to less than half their net previous earnings in work.[5]

The effects of inadequate benefit levels were demonstrated in Richard Berthoud's study for the DHSS, on the basis of which he concluded: 'With the possible exception of the down-and-out homeless, direct measures of hardship show there is no poorer group of people than unemployed couples with children.'[6]

Not surprisingly, debt is a serious problem for many unemployed people, and the doubling of unemployment between 1980 and 1981 was shadowed by the doubling of Actions entered for mortgage possession between 1980 and 1984. Burgoyne, in a recent study of the effect of unemployment on married life, found a marked difference in levels of home-ownership with length of unemployment, suggesting that many of those out of work for more than two years had already sold up and moved into rented accommodation.[7]

Unemployment and health
Low benefit income can also seriously affect family health, and babies with unemployed fathers tend to have a lower birthweight than babies with fathers in work. There is also evidence that children of unemployed fathers tend to be shorter than those of employed fathers.[8]

Moser, Fox, Jones and Goldblatt, analysing OPCS longitudinal data, found a higher than normal death rate among unemployed men and their wives over the period 1971-81. The authors infer from their findings that as the effects on health of a drop in income and increased stress build up, there is a real increase in mortality.[9] Scott-Samuel, applying the results obtained by Moser et al to the unemployment levels of 1984, suggests that the average annual unemployment attributable mortality is in the region of 2,125 men and 1,077 of their wives.[10]

While the paucity of research on the subject means that the causal link between unemployment and loss of physical health is contentious, the damaging psychological effects of unemployment are well established. Speaking in December 1984, the then health minister Kenneth Clarke acknowledged: 'I've never been in any doubts that our present grave problems of unemployment do indeed add to the health problems of the nation.'[11]

A dramatic manifestation of this link between unemployment and health was recorded by Platt and Kreitman in their study of parasuicide and unemployment in Edinburgh, 1968-82. Their findings clearly associate unemployment and parasuicide rates among Edinburgh males. This association was 'positive and highly significant over time and across geographical areas of the city. More crucially, throughout the period the parasuicide rate among the unemployed was considerably higher than the rate among the employed.'[12]

Smith, referring to Warr, lists nine ways in which unemployment can damage mental health: first, as a result of financial worries; second, as a consequence of the 'restricted behaviours and environments' of the unemployed once they have lost the social contact of the workplace and can't afford leisure activities that will maintain or establish social contacts; third, they lose 'traction': the momentum that the structure of work provides; fourth, unemployed people have a smaller scope for making decisions – it is difficult for unemployed people to make decisions that will greatly affect their lives because they don't have the necessary material resources; fifth, unemployed people lose many of the opportunities to obtain satisfaction through the exercise of existing skills and the learning of new ones; sixth, there is an increase in threatening and humiliating experiences, typified by repeated unsuccessful job applications, confrontations with unsympathetic officials, being regarded as a failure or a scrounger; seventh, there is increased anxiety about the future; eighth, there is a decline in the quality of interpersonal contacts; ninth, there is a decline in social position.[13]

Exchequer cost of unemployment[14]

Just as unemployment can impose severe economic and social costs on individuals and families, it also imposes considerable costs on the wider community.

A high level of unemployment in a community means that less money than before is available to be spent locally. Demand for goods and services falls, and firms lay off staff or go into liquidation. This means a further loss of local spending power and more job losses and the area becomes increasingly run-down and inhospitable to local economic activity. While easy to recognise, this effect is difficult to quantify.

More easily quantifiable is the exchequer cost of unemployment in Great Britain: the costs of benefit payments to the unemployed, the cost of foregone direct and indirect tax revenue and lost national insurance contributions.

Benefit payments to the unemployed in the financial year 1986/7 are estimated to total £7,420 million, or £2,269 for every unemployed benefit claimant.[15] The cost of administering these benefits is given as £2.50 per week for unemployment benefit and £3.05 per week in the case of SB claimants.[16] The number of unemployed benefit recipients during the year 1986/7 is estimated at 725,000 drawing UB only, 1,890,000 drawing SB only, and 225,000 drawing UB plus SB. This implies a total expenditure of £426.5 million during 1986/7, or £130 per unemployed benefit claimant. There is also the cost of an estimated 54,400 unemployed men aged 60 and over taken out of the official claimant figures because they are entitled to the long-term SB rate. This is estimated to add a further £47 per unemployed

claimant. Expenditure from the redundancy fund is expected to total £189 million in 1986/7, or £58 per unemployed claimant.[17] Total benefit and redundancy costs borne by the exchequer in 1986/7 are therefore estimated at £2,504 per unemployed claimant.

Forgone income tax less tax deducted from unemployment benefits will come to approximately £1,793 per unemployed claimant (calculated using the assumptions adopted by Sinfield and Fraser, that the average earnings of the unemployed while in work are only 80 per cent of average earnings, and that income tax comes to 23 per cent of gross pay). Sinfield and Fraser's estimate of lost national insurance contributions in 1985 came to £1,625 per unemployed claimant, which updated to 1986/7 is equal to £1,700, in line with Whitfield's estimate.[18]

The calculation of indirect tax assumes that unemployed people spend 90 per cent of their disposable income when in work, and that they spend all their benefit when out of work. The rate of all indirect taxes on spending is assumed to amount to 20 per cent, and 25 per cent of the unemployed are assumed to maintain their pre-unemployment income by drawing on savings and redundancy payments and by falling into debt. This suggests an indirect tax loss of £560 per unemployed claimant in 1986/7.

Totalling these items, the exchequer cost of unemployment resulting from the cost of benefit payments to the unemployed, lost direct and indirect taxes and lost national insurance contributions comes to £6,557 a year for every unemployed benefit claimant – a total of more than £21 billion a year at current unemployment levels. This figure, of course, ignores the private and community costs of unemployment already mentioned. It also ignores the substantial cost of unemployment borne by local authorities, the personal social services, the health service, and the Manpower Services Commission in its special employment and training schemes.

Defining away the problem

The extent of unemployment in the UK has been obscured in recent years by the large number of changes to the official unemployment count. Prior to November 1982 the monthly count was based on the number of people registered for work at Jobcentres and Careers Offices. In November 1982 this was changed to a count of unemployed benefit claimants, with the result that over 170,000 people were, conveniently for the government, removed from the statistics.

Because the official unemployment count only includes benefit claimants, administrative changes to benefit regulations or changes in the eligibility criteria for special employment measures can substantially reduce it without a single additional job being created. In total, the unemployment count has undergone some 19 changes since 1979, and some of the more important ones are listed in the Table.

	Change	Estimated effect on monthly count*
Oct 1982	Change in definition and compilation of monthly unemployment figures from a clerical count of people registered for work at Jobcentres and careers offices to a computer count covering only benefit claimants	–170,000 to –190,000 In addition: estimated effect on number of school-leavers recorded –26,000**
Apr 1983	Men aged 60+ and not entitled to benefit no longer required to sign on at benefit offices in order to get NI credits.	–107,400 by June 1983
June 1983	All men aged 60+ allowed long-term SB rate as soon as they come on to SB	–54,400 by Aug 1983
June 1983	As a result of provision introduced in November 1980 barring school-leavers from claiming benefit until Sept each year, together with change in monthly count to claimants only in Oct 1982, between 100,000 and 200,000 unemployed school-leavers are missed from the monthly figures for June, July and Aug each year.	–100,000 to –200,000
Oct 1984	Change in CP eligibility rules. Entry now limited to unemployed benefit claimants.	–29,000 by Jan 1986**
Mar 1986	Introduction of a two-week delay in publication of monthly unemployment count 'to improve accuracy'.	between –40,000 and –90,000, average –50,000
June 1986	New method of calculating unemployment rate, using larger denominator. Initially this was published alongside rate calculated on old basis, but from Sept 1986 count has now replaced it.	–1 to –1.5 percentage points (mostly –1.4)
Oct 1986	Abolition of right to half and three-quarter rate unemployment benefit for people with insufficient NI contributions to qualify for full rate (decision announced on 15 Jan 1986).	–24,000 after 1 year; –30,000 after 2 years**
end Oct 1986 - Jan 1987	Introduction of tighter availability for work test.	–95,000 after 1 year; –120,000 after 2 years**

* Estimated effects are those published by the Department of Employment except where marked.
** Estimated effect derived from Department of Employment, DHSS or Treasury data by Unemployment Unit.

The aggregate effect of recent unemployment count changes is to reduce the non-seasonally adjusted 'headline' total by about 450,000 (increased to about 550,000 in June, July and August by the removal of summer school-leavers from the count). These figures take no account of the growth of special employment and training measures, which in December 1986 covered 729,383 people, and had the effect of further reducing the unemployment figure by over 550,000.

This means that without special employment and training measures and recent changes to the unemployment count, the official monthly unemployment total would be about 1 million higher than it is currently.

Special measures

Although it would be wrong to suggest that all these changes have been introduced with the sole intention of massaging the unemployment figures, it is difficult to believe that the effect has been altogether unwelcome to the government.

Statistical changes and special employment and training measures seem to constitute the two major planks of the government's response to unemployment. The number of people covered by special measures has risen from 260,000 in Autumn 1978, with an annual cost of £490 million, to 729,383 in December 1986. The MSC's estimated expenditure for the year 1986/7 is £2,968.9 million.

The two most disturbing trends over the period have been the steady running down of real training opportunities (matched by an increase in training rhetoric) and an increasingly crude use of schemes to lever down the pay and expectations of the low paid.

The Community Programme – currently one of the MSC's most important measures for the adult unemployed – has little training provision. The new Job Training Scheme (JTS), in spite of its name, appears to offer little quality training, and is being financed by the diversion of resources from the MSC's other Adult Training Strategy programmes and a planned underspend on the Community Programme and YTS. YTS – now stretched into a two-year programme – continues to offer a combination of training and 'work experience' of patchy quality. Meanwhile, TOPS courses are being trimmed, and 29 skillcentres have been closed since 1984. Following the winding up of 16 Industrial Training Boards the number of conventional apprenticeship places has shrunk to virtual insignificance, and the obstacle of the DHSS's 21-hour rule still discourages unemployed people from undertaking conventional college-based training or education for recognised qualifications.

Workfare

The new JTS and the recently introduced Restart Programme represent the MSC's adoption of many elements of the American Workfare, the main features of which are compulsory working for benefits, motivation courses and enforced job search. Under Restart, by April 1987 1.3 million long-term unemployed claimants will have been interviewed, and from that date everyone out of work for six months or more will be called to a Jobcentre for a Restart interview every six months until they have been unemployed for three years.

Once called for interview claimants are required to make a selection from a menu of options. These include attending a job interview (rare, and only 1 per cent of interviewees are actually placed in jobs); training (subject to the 21-hour rule if a normal college course); attending an interview for a place on the Community Programme; Jobstart (financial incentive to accept a low-paid job); New Workers Scheme (a subsidy to employers to offer low paid work); attending a Jobclub (help with job applications); entering a Restart Course (re-motivation course), and JTS (working for benefits). Significantly, Restart and JTS are being implemented against a background of a more stringent availability for work test for unemployed claimants, and tougher benefit sanctions for those who refuse suitable opportunities or leave work or training voluntarily.

Clearly, neither Restart nor JTS can create new jobs for unemployed people. The assumptions behind them are twofold. First, the less thoughtful of Workfare's UK advocates seem to believe that sufficient jobs already exist for unemployed people if only they can be motivated to apply for them, or render themselves employable by undergoing low level training. The fact that the Department of Employment's own estimates indicate that for the UK as a whole, there are six unemployed benefit claimants chasing every existing job vacancy, coupled with the fact that many of these vacancies are for part-time work while most unemployed claimants want and need full-time jobs, demonstrates the weakness of this argument.

A second, more cynical justification for a Workfare approach is that forcing unemployed people to work for benefits will inevitably undermine wages and employment conditions of the low paid workers they threaten to replace, thereby helping to hold down the rate of pay increases.

The problem here is that New Earnings Survey data show that, in general, pay increases among the low paid have not been inflationary – in fact, as chapter 4 shows, many low paid workers have suffered real wage reductions since 1978. The most inflationary increases have been enjoyed by such groups as finance, insurance and tax specialists, policemen, office managers, accountants, and personnel and industrial relations managers. Wage reductions among the low paid, however swingeing, will be unlikely to influence these groups.

Future prospects

An Unemployment Unit study of the 'Jobs gap' suggests that the equivalent of four million new full-time jobs need to be created in Britain in order to

provide paid employment for everyone wanting work. This figure takes full account of the Department of Employment's estimate of the number of existing vacancies in the economy.[19] If the rate of job creation experienced between September 1985 and September 1986 is maintained, *it will take 30 years to provide a job for everyone wanting one, and at least 15 years to bring unemployment back down to one million.* All studies show that a person's chance of finding work falls sharply with length of time unemployed. This means that as the number of available jobs increases, many of the long-term unemployed will remain at the back of the queue.

The situation is exacerbated by the fact that expected future demand for employees is likely to centre on professional based occupations; technicians; multi-skilled craftsmen; and support and personal service occupations involving part-time work. The number of unskilled full-time jobs is expected to fall significantly.[20] Yet unskilled and unqualified workers are disproportionately represented among the long-term unemployed.

Neither statistical manipulation nor Workfare based schemes will solve this problem. Only serious efforts to increase the economy's capacity to employ people, coupled with a dramatic increase in the availability of genuine training and education opportunities, with access and encouragement for the unemployed, hold out any hope for the future. In the meantime, the devastating personal costs of unemployment *can* be quickly eased by raising benefit rates above their present punitive levels.

CHAPTER 9

Poor health

Peter Townsend

The inextricable relationship between ill-health and poverty is likely to grow in political significance throughout the remainder of this century. This will be not just because of rising public interest in the consequences for life-styles for health, or growing support for 'Green' policies. It will be because of increasing concern about inequalities of health, and the increasing capacity of medical scientists, epidemiologists and other social scientists to unravel the causes of those inequalities and show how they can be countered.

Exposing inequalities in health

The disturbing trends in health first gained widespread public attention in 1980. In 1977 a working group headed by Sir Douglas Black had been set up by the then secretary of state for social services, David Ennals, to review evidence about differences in health status among the social classes, identify possible causes and draw out the implications for policy as well as for further research. At that time the health of the British population was not improving on some indicators quite as fast as that of a number of other industrial societies. For example, although in 1960 the infant mortality rates of countries like Finland and France were much higher than the rate for the United Kingdom, by the mid-1970s they were much lower. And, despite strong support for the National Health Service (NHS), and especially for the principle of equal access to health care irrespective of income, on which the service is based, one research paper after another pointed out that inequalities in health between classes remained wide.

Early in 1980 the working group submitted its report to the incoming secretary of state of a new government, Patrick Jenkin. He was not very pleased. The report ran counter to the whole of the Thatcher government's philosophy of cutting public expenditure and leaving the choice of priorities to the market and to the power of the family purse. The secretary of state published the report later that year, on a Friday evening before the August bank holiday, under a short preface which described the cost of meeting the recommendations in the report as 'quite unrealistic in present or any foreseeable economic circumstances, quite apart from any

82

judgement that may be formed of the effectiveness of such expenditure in dealing with the problems identified'. Copies of the report were scarce, because only 260 had been printed by the DHSS.[1]

Nonetheless, the report attracted, and continues to attract, the interest of a large number of doctors and others concerned with health in Britain and many countries overseas. Many summaries were produced for different audiences and many conferences were called in the United Kingdom and in Europe.[2]

Interest in the report appeared to have built up for a number of reasons. The problem of measuring the extent and distribution of a problem was related to scientific explanation, and such explanation was regarded as vital to the formulation, or indeed re-formulation of policy. For the first time a study of the development of a nation's health was placed at the heart of both the evaluation and construction of health care policies. The income groups and the occupation and family groups in the worst situations could be identified. The high health standards achieved by some social groups could be properly regarded as attainable by others.

An obligation to provide a scientific explanation for inequalities in health is bound to lead to a better definition of responsibilities for a nation's health – especially the balance of responsibilities as between the health care services and other social institutions – like housing, education, industry, agriculture and environmental health. Social and not just individual health has to be defined, measured and explained.

The working group under Sir Douglas Black found that epidemiological, sociological and medical research had not progressed to the point of permitting the causes of poor health in the population to be spelt out very precisely. This was partly a problem of inadequate theory, but also of the wrongly balanced funding and development of research. There were too few examples of population or longitudinal research studies, and of these being related to policy. The implications for health of different material and social experiences of individuals, classes and local communities had yet to be disentangled and exactly quantified. Indeed, this shortcoming in the capacity to analyse the reasons for the unequal distribution of health in populations represented, and continues to represent, a major research challenge for all the sciences concerned with health. A concerted research strategy, aimed at cutting unnecessary premature deaths and rapidly promoting good health, was recommended, but completely ignored by the government – even though this represented a small fraction of the costs of the proposals put forward by Sir Douglas Black's group. That programme continues to require urgent development.

Health and poverty

However, despite the provisional or general nature of the evidence which was then available, the Black working group drew unequivocal conclusions about the direction of that evidence. It found that material deprivation played the major role in explaining the very unfavourable health record of the poorer sections of the population – especially of the partly skilled and unskilled manual groups making up more than a quarter of the entire population – with biological cultural and personal life-style factors playing a contributory role.

This conclusion carried a powerful implication for the construction of policy. If inequalities in health were to be tackled, the elimination or reduction of material deprivation and not just the organisation of more efficient health care services had to become a national objective for action. Policies external to the NHS were, therefore, of crucial importance if inequalities were to be reduced and Britain's health performance radically improved. Low wages and minimum social security and child benefits had to be raised. Poor housing and environmental conditions had to be improved. A big programme of improvement in the services for elderly people and those with disabilities had to be developed and in many other respects the two nations drawn much closer together.

The report also called attention to the face that insufficient attention was being paid to the need to promote healthier life-styles more equally among the population. There were financial, education and other restrictions on the opportunities of some groups to achieve such life-styles. This tended to sharpen health inequalities in Britain.

In the seven years since the report was submitted new evidence about mortality and other aspects of health has been published, and a number of the propositions, both scientific and practical, in that report have been examined publicly. Some elements in the discussion – like the relationship between unemployment and health, the renewed concern with housing, the evidence of great social polarisation, the changes taking place in the diet and life-styles of millions of people, if not yet a majority of the population – are of enormous public interest and are important too for any understanding of patterns of health and the choice of health policies.

The widening health divide

In March 1987 the Health Education Council (HEC) issued an updating of the 1980 Black Report, entitled *The Health Divide*.[3] Compiled by Margaret Whitehead, this showed that the health gap is continuing to widen. The health of the professional, administrative and managerial classes continues to improve. The so-called diseases of affluence have virtually disappeared. The exceptions are cancer of the skin and, for women only, cancer of the brain, of the breast and of the bone marrow. But the health of the poorest quarter of the population has improved very little. *Rates of death in middle life, among men and women, are nearly as bad as they were thirty or forty years ago and there are a few diseases where the problem is worse.*

The publication provoked a major row. The Chairman of the Council, Sir

Brian Bailey, tried to stop the Press launch because he anticipated that the report would not be received with much enthusiasm by the government. The fact is that the scientific message is even sharper than it was in 1980 and can be expressed with greater authority and depth.

For one thing, the 'health divide' appears to be larger in Britain than in some other industrial countries and, contrary to experience elsewhere, has been *widening* rather than remaining roughly the same or getting narrower. This means that Britain's health record over recent decades compares unfavourably with countries like France and Finland, where striking improvements have taken place. On health indicators, Britain has been slipping down the world charts.

Furthermore, there is evidence reinforcing the conclusion that although genes and life-styles play their part, the dominant cause of inequalities in health and premature death is *material deprivation*. Thus, some forms of respiratory disease have been traced to spores from fungae in damp and dilapidated housing. There has been a lot of work revealing the role of pollutants, especially air-borne metal particles, in areas of the inner city and communities bordering industrial plants. The strong relationship between premature death and deprivation has been followed through into old age in the longitudinal survey of census households by Professor John Fox and his colleagues at the City University. Inadequate incomes in old age and among young families with new babies have been shown to underlie the risk of getting hypothermia, which is a more common condition in Britain than in many other countries. The effects of mass unemployment have been traced not only to mental stress, depression and suicide but to physical diseases – like stomach ulcers. There is strong evidence of shortages of food among low income families and of their inability to afford some food stuffs like fresh fruit and vegetables at certain times of the year.[4]

Bad housing, bad environmental conditions and facilities, bad working conditions, unemployment and above all inadequate income – these are the elements in the material conditions of life which help to demonstrate the impact of material deprivation.

Some of the latest international as well as British studies on incomes and small areas drive home the scientific message. Thus, *after* standardising for smoking, alcohol consumption, physical exercise and other behavioural or life-style factors, the risk of premature death in Alameda county in California remained 60 per cent higher among those with 'inadequate' incomes compared with those with 'very adequate' incomes. In Britain Professor Michael Marmot has obtained a similar kind of result in his work on different salary grades of the Civil Service.[5] And a study of 678 wards in the North of England found that indicators of material deprivation 'explained' as much as 65 per cent of the variation of mortality, permanent sickness or disability and babies with low birthweight.[6]

This national problem was developing under previous governments but has accelerated since 1979. The number of homeless, even excluding the single homeless, has grown by 100,000. More rented, especially council, accommodation has fallen into disrepair. According to the government's Family Expenditure Survey, the real disposable incomes of the richest quarter of the population have grown significantly, while the real incomes of the poorest quarter have actually gone down. This is a consequence not only of a massive increase in unemployment but of lower wage-levels at the bottom of the labour market, the removal of earnings-related unemployment and sickness benefits, other reductions in social security, and pinch-penny school meals and child welfare policies. The government's failure to promote effective inner-city and anti-racist programmes, as urged, for example, by the report of the Archbishop of Canterbury's Commission, *Faith in the City*, has contributed to the impoverishment of already deprived areas.

An anti-poverty policy for health

The World Health Organisation Regional Office for Europe has set targets for 'Health for All' by the year 2000 which were endorsed in 1984 by all European member countries, including Britain. The first of the 38 targets in the programme is equity in health. The target for greater equity is defined as to bring about a reduction of at least 25 per cent in the differences in health status between groups and countries, by improving the health of disadvantaged groups.

Britain has failed so far to define its target operationally. One possible interpretation of the meaning of that target would be to cut the annual number of deaths among persons under the pensionable ages in the poorer manual groups by some 20,000 in the last year of the century. Another implication of the programme would be to cut the likely number of chronically sick and disabled people under the pensionable ages in the poorer manual groups at the end of the century by approximately 100,000.

The policies would have to be a mixture of central and local policies to improve substandard housing, raise minimum wages and at the same time attack unsafe and deprived working conditions, redistribute a higher proportion of resources to pensioners and other social security beneficiaries, increase child benefit, encourage a big fall in tobacco and alcohol consumption, partly by trimming the power of the tobacco and drink lobbies in Parliament and elsewhere, and a variety of supporting measures to equalise living standards and transform the conditions of deprived sections of the population.

On the basis of the latest data from the social and medical sciences, as listed in the HEC report, but also on the basis of the latest information about the distribution of resources, these kinds of objectives are attainable. For example, there is abundant evidence of the polarisation of earnings and of other income under the Conservative government (see chapter 4). In principle, the incomes of the poorest quarter of the population could be doubled if as little as £1 in £6 of the disposable incomes of the richest quartile could gradually be transferred to them. Britain remains a prosperous society and, as argued in chapter 15, a modest programme of redistribution could dramatically reduce material deprivation.

Conclusion

The World Health Organisation recognises that the objective of greater equity is a daunting one which, though theoretically viable, is not likely to be pursued without very radical change. The undertaking to reduce health inequalities by at least 25 per cent will remain an empty gesture unless the governments can be persuaded or compelled to seek better information, undertake large-scale experiments, introduce anti-poverty policies, give priority to healthier life-styles and monitor the effects of those experiments and policies on the health of the population as a whole, and on the health of the poorest groups in particular. A new health warning deserves to be publicised on every hoarding, in every newspaper and on every TV programme: Poverty damages health; poverty kills.

CHAPTER 10

What happened to spending on the welfare state?

John Hills

'Public expenditure is at the heart of Britain's present economic difficulties.' So began the government's first policy statement on public spending in November 1979.[1] Public spending was supposed to have reduced economic growth relative to that of other industrialised countries, to have fuelled inflation and to have led to ruinous taxation which had destroyed incentives to the 'wealth-producing' sectors of the economy. Accordingly, the government set about making cuts, confident that by reducing the level of public spending it would liberate resources for the private sector, reduce the tax burden and make inroads into the unemployment total–then standing at 1.2 million.

There is no doubt that the government *wanted* to cut public spending. Nor is there any doubt that many services *have* been cut. What is at first paradoxical is that public spending has indisputably *increased* under the Conservatives (and the tax burden with it). Even after allowing for inflation, public spending in 1986/7 was some 14 per cent higher than it had been in 1978/9, the last year of the Labour government.

Public spending as a share of national income

If one knew nothing of the history of the last eight years such an increase would be unsurprising. After all, allowing again for inflation, national income has grown at an annual average rate of 1.6 per cent since 1978/9. This may not be very impressive beside the average of 2.6 per cent during the 25 years of 'economic decline' which monetarism was supposed to reverse, but it does mean that the economy is 13.5 per cent larger than it was in 1978/9. *The proportion of national income which is spent by the public sector is, therefore, very much the same as it was when the Conservatives took over in 1979.*

There are many reasons why this might be expected to happen. For instance, it might be thought reasonable that pensioners should share in the growing wealth of the community. To achieve this state pensions would be increased in line with the growth of the economy; linking them to earnings would have much the same effect. Spending on pensions would grow more

88

quickly than prices, but the share of national income they represented would stay the same (unless the number of pensioners changed). Similarly, we might expect the earnings of those working in the public sector, such as nurses and doctors, to keep pace with earnings elsewhere. With the same numbers employed, the public sector wage bill would then represent a constant share of national income.

The changing pattern of public spending

Having lived through it, we know that the past eight years have not been quite like that. Pensions have not been kept up with earnings. Nor, as David Piachaud shows in chapter 3, have benefit levels kept up. Public sector wages have, in many cases, fallen behind those in the rest of the economy and manpower numbers have been cut. The constant level of spending as a share of national income does *not* represent the results of a gradually growing total of unchanged composition, but the almost accidental result of the collision between exploding *needs* for services as the economy has dived into recession and the government's attempts to cut back levels of provision in selected areas.

Table 1: *UK public expenditure 1978/9 to 1986/7*
(£bn, 1986/7 prices)

	78/9	83/4	86/7	Percentage growth 78/9 to 86/7
Social security	34.2	41.8	46.5	+36
Education	17.6	18.0	18.7	+ 6
Health	15.1	17.6	18.8	+24
Defence	14.6	17.6	18.6	+28
Housing	8.8	5.0	4.0	–55
Personal social services	2.8	3.2	3.5	+28
Overseas aid	1.4	1.2	1.2	–15
Other*	33.7	34.3	34.6	+ 3
Total	128.0	138.6	145.9	+14
National income	334.8	348.5	380.1	+14

* Does not include debt interest and does not include privatisation as negative spending.
Sources: All figures from *The government's expenditure plans 1983-4 to 1985-6* (Cmnd 8789) and *1987-88 to 1989-90* (Cm 56). Figures are on a UK basis incorporating relevant portions of territorial spending, and have been adjusted to give consistency of coverage over the period as explained in the text. Adjustment to 1986/7 prices is by reference to GDP (market prices) deflator.

Table 1 shows what happened to some of the main components of the public spending total between 1978/9 and 1983/4, and between then and 1986/7. The widely varying experiences of the different programmes are shown clearly. At one extreme, the housing budget has been more than halved in real terms, while at the other, the social security budget has increased by more than a third. An unsurprising 'winner' has been the defence programme, up by 28 per cent. More surprising, on the face of it, is the fact that the health and personal social services budgets have enjoyed increases at almost the same rate. The share of national resources put into education is down, with the programme's real growth rate half that of national income. Meanwhile, despite an overall increase in living standards, the amount spent on overseas aid is down 15 per cent in real terms, giving a clear indication of the government's attitude to the poor in the rest of the world.

The social security programme

The real increase in the cost of social security – more than £12 billion since 1978/9 – might perhaps be taken as an indication that the government had decided that charity begins at home; that is, until we look at the detailed figures.

Table 2: *Social security spending 1978/9 to 1986/7*
(£b, 1986/7 prices)

	78/9	83/4	86/7	Percentage growth 78/9 to 86/7
Pensions	17.1	18.7	19.7	+ 16
Child benefit	4.9	4.7	4.7	– 4
Sickness, disability, etc.	4.2	4.7	5.8	+ 38
Supplementary benefit	3.2	6.7	8.4	+161
Housing benefit	1.8	3.2	3.8	+113
Unemployment benefit	1.3	1.8	1.8	+ 39
Other family benefits	0.3	0.3	0.3	– 7
Administration	1.5	1.8	2.0	+ 36
Total	34.2	41.8	46.5	+ 36

Sources: As table 1. Categories adjusted on to consistent basis as described in text.

Table 3: *Numbers receiving main benefits 1978/9 to 1986/7 (000s)*

	78/9	83/4	86/7	Percentage growth 78/9 to 86/7
Child benefit*	13,968	13,132	12,717	– 9
Retirement pension	8,711	9,408	9,782	+12
Housing benefit**	3,510	4,883	5,072	+45
Supplementary benefit	3,140	4,610	5,084	+62
Unemployment benefit	600	1,054	975	+63
Invalidity benefit†	600	760	915	+53

* Number of children.
** Assistance with *rent* only; GB figures; 1978/9 figures include tenants on SB (from *Social Security Statistics* 1984).
† GB figures.
Sources As table 1

Table 2 shows a breakdown of the social security programme into its main parts, while table 3 shows some simple indicators of the levels of need for the idfferent kinds of spending.

Pensions

Spending on pensions (of all kinds, including widows' benefits, the state retirement pension and the new earnings related component) is the largest part of the programme – by itself equivalent to more than 5 per cent of national income. Its real level is over 15 per cent higher than in 1978/9, a slightly faster rate of growth than public spending overall or of national income. This does not result from an attempt to keep payments to pensioners up with the rise in general living standards, however. One of the government's first acts was to break the link between pensions and earnings, pledging itself only to keep their value up with prices. What has happened – as table 3 shows – is that there are 12 per cent more pensioners than there were. *Spending per pensioner has hardly changed in real terms.*

It is true that some pensioners now receive more from private occupational pension schemes than in the past – as a result of their own contributions – and that the 1975 state earnings related pension scheme (SERPS) has begun to bear some fruit. But this is little comfort for those whose main source of income is the basic retirement pension. The increase in real spending on pensions is almost entirely accounted for by demography; the level of spending per pensioner has steadily fallen behind the growth of national prosperity, and has only just kept ahead of prices. Thus a pensioner couple are £11.30 a week worse off than they would have been if the government had not changed the method of uprating pensions.[2]

Child benefit
The next largest component of the social security programme used to be child benefit (that is, if, as in the tables in this chapter, the equivalent of the child tax allowances for income tax which still existed in 1978/9 are counted as child benefit in that year in order to give a fair comparison over time). Over the period as a whole, real spending on child benefit fell by 3.5 per cent. It should be noted, however, that there are 9 per cent fewer children than there used to be. Spending per child is, therefore, up 6 per cent – that is, it has increased at less than half the rate of real national income. Spending on child benefit has also fallen behind the growth of national prosperity, although spending per child has kept ahead of prices, despite the cut in child benefit's real value.

Other family benefits – family income supplement (FIS), maternity allowance, maternity grant and one-parent benefit – are a much smaller part of the total, and one which is shrinking as rates of benefit fall behind inflation. Their combined total is down 6.5 per cent in real terms. This has happened while the numbers on FIS and one-parent benefit have more than doubled, and the number receiving maternity allowance has been constant. Despite the rapid increase in the numbers of recipients, spending on other family benefits has fallen behind inflation, let alone national income.

Sickness, disability, invalidity and injuries benefits
Looking at movements in the total of these benefits is complicated by the creative accounting which the government has used in order to try to reassure its own supporters that public spending is not really rising. From 1983/4 a large chunk of what had been sickness benefit was handed over to employers, who deducted the cost from what they would otherwise have had to pay in tax. This magically reduced the level of public spending, even though it made little difference to the overall balance of the government's finances. In order to give a fair comparison with 1978/9, the cost of this 'tax expenditure' – employers' statutory sick pay – has been added back into the totals for 1983/4 and 1986/7.

With this adjustment there is a significant increase in the real level of expenditure – 38 per cent over the whole period. This is, however, a smaller increase than in the number of recipients of the main item of spending in this area, invalidity benefit, which has grown by 50 per cent. It is not easy to say how much of the increase in the numbers receiving these benefits is due to the effects of rising unemployment and how much to genuinely increased coverage, but very little of the increase in the level of spending is due to any increase in the generosity of individual benefits, and in some cases the benefits have been cut (see chapter 12).

Supplementary benefits
Spending on supplementary benefit (SB) rose by 160 per cent in real terms between 1978/9 and 1986/7 (excluding the payments of recipients' rents in 1978/9 which are included with housing benefits below to give a fair comparison with the current system). As readers will already be aware from chapter 3, this does not relate to an increase in the relative generosity of the scale rates; whether they have kept up with an appropriate measure of prices is debatable, but they have certainly fallen well behind the living standards of the population as a whole.

The total number of SB recipients has risen by 62 per cent. This is, however, the result of a fairly constant number of pensioners receiving relatively small top-ups to their other incomes (such as the state retirement pension) combined with an increase of 150 per cent in the number of non-pensioner recipients. Non-pensioners, particularly the unemployed on the short-term rates, typically have very few other resources and therefore receive rather larger amounts of SB. The increase in the cost of SB is no more than a reflection of the vast increase in unemployment. *The level of spending for each (non-pensioner) recipient has fallen behind prices, let alone overall national income*, even though the rates have risen faster than the general retail price index (a poor measure of the impact of inflation on benefit recipients.)

Housing benefits
Spending on housing benefits (including the 1978/9 equivalents of what are now counted as 'certificated' housing benefit) more than doubled in real terms over the period. The number of recipients of assistance with rent increased by only 45 per cent, so there was a significant increase in spending per case. This was no more, however, than a reflection of the massive increase in local authority rents – by nearly 50 per cent in real terms between 1980 and 1982.

The increase in the cost of housing benefits has little or nothing to do with the administrative upheaval when the scheme was dumped on the local authorities; it mostly results from the rent increases pre-dating the switch. This is the direct consequence of the government's use of the new housing subsidy system to cut current spending on general subsidies within the housing programme. Given the numbers either receiving 100 per cent assistance with rent because they are on SB, or partial assistance because they are on standard housing benefit (the numbers of whom increase with higher rents), just under *half* of the Department of the Environment's 'saving' from higher rents will have emerged directly as increased cost to the DHSS's housing benefit programme.

The value of the needs allowances and the other rules which determine the actual levels of housing benefit have become *less* generous over the period. Together, the increase in the number of recipients – another function of growing poverty and unemployment as well as higher rents – and higher rents themselves more than account for higher real spending on housing benefits.

Unemployment benefit

It is, at first sight, surprising that the cost of unemployment benefit has only risen by 40 per cent while unemployment has tripled. Most of the unemployed do not receive unemployment benefit, however. As long-term and youth unemployment have increased, a lower and lower proportion of the unemployed have been entitled to receive a contribution based benefit which lasts only one year. With the abolition of earnings related supplement and the abolition of the child additions, fewer people have found that their unemployment benefit entitlement lifts them clear of SB levels. As a result, the number of recipients has only risen by 63 per cent, despite mass unemployment. The increase in the cost of unemployment benefit has – as a result of less generous rates of benefit – been less than the increase in the number of claimants; it is SB which has carried the bulk of the cost of unemployment.

Social security as a whole

The cost of administering the programme has increased at exactly the same rate – 36 per cent – as that of the programme as a whole. As the growth of the programme represents a much larger number of people receiving, in some cases, less generous benefits (and not more money going to the same number of people), this also reflects a reduction in the resources available relative to the increasing needs. This finding will come as no surprise to both desperate staff in inner-city DHSS and housing benefit offices and angry and frustrated claimants who have to wait for hours in appalling conditions.

The DHSS's own analysis of changes in social security spending, prepared on a rather different basis from the rest of this chapter, shows that about two-thirds of the real growth in spending between 1978/9 and 1986/7 can be ascribed to the increased number of claimants – particularly unemployed claimants.[3] The remaining third is attributable to real increases in the average amounts of benefit paid, which is not necessarily the same thing as real increases in benefit levels. For example, part of this increase reflects higher rents feeding through into housing benefit payments and part the lower incomes of those coming on to SB compared with in earlier years. Thus, only a small proportion of the overall increase can be ascribed to actual improvements in benefits, and even then these improvements have not been sufficient to keep up with a general rise in living standards.

Overall, the increased spending on the social security system does not reflect more generous benefit levels; quite the reverse in a number of cases. For most parts of the programme, spending per recipient has fallen behind prices, even where benefit levels have risen faster than the RPI. And most important, in terms of claimants' share of national wealth, even where both spending per recipient and benefit levels have edged ahead of prices, they have, in virtually all cases, fallen well behind the growth rates of earnings or national income as a whole. The increase in real spending can mainly be ascribed to increased numbers of claimants, which are, in turn, mainly attributable to increased unemployment and demographic changes.

Spending on health[4]

What has happened to spending on the health service is the subject of a well rehearsed argument. As table 1 shows, real spending on health was up 24 per cent over the period, representing an *increased* share of national resources going in this direction. It is this statistic which the government regularly uses to claim that 'the health service is safe with us'. However, the statistic appears to be completely at variance with the widespread public *perception* that the resources available to the NHS are declining.

There are several factors to bear in mind. First, we need to take account of the rising real costs of labour intensive services. Spending on such services has to rise faster than prices just to keep still. The exact calculation depends on the pay of health workers relative to the rest of the community. Similarly, it is the cost of special items like drugs which matters, rather than of goods in general as measured by the RPI. Using a specific 'NHS deflator' suggests that the *volume* of health services provided by government rose by only 5 per cent over the period 1978/9 to 1983/4, as opposed to the 16 per cent increase in their real *cost* over the same period shown in table 1. Since then there has been little rise in the volume of services provided.

This still means that there has been an apparent *increase* in the total volume of services provided, not the perceived decline. We then have to take account of the *need* for spending. The number of elderly people – especially the very elderly with particularly high needs for health services – has been rising rapidly. The DHSS's own index of the 'demographic demand' for health services has been increasing by 0.7 per cent every year. On top of that the government has said that additional spending of 0.5 per cent a year is needed to keep up with medical advances and the demand for the health service to do things which it could not do before. Together, these factors are of much the same size as the growth in the volume of services.

Finally, there has been a shift of resources *within* the health service – both towards regions which have been starved of resources in the past, and towards the 'Cinderella services' (such as services for the mentally ill and for the elderly). This shift has meant fewer resources for previously well-endowed regions (such as London) and for well-favoured services (such as teaching hospitals). Some of the most visible – and vocal – parts of the NHS have found out what it is like to be reduced towards the level of the rest.

In total, health spending has risen more rapidly than either prices or national income. In relation to its own costs the increase is much smaller, however, and this increase has been barely enough – if that – to keep up with the rising needs of an ageing population and medical advances. Combined with the reallocation of resources within the NHS, this has meant a *fall* in the level of resources available to many of the services with which the public comes most often into contact. Here, the level of service is perceived as declining because it *is* declining, notwithstanding the overall increase in spending.

Housing

Of all the areas of welfare state spending, it is housing which has been hardest hit over the last eight years, with the budget down by more than a half in real terms over the period (even ignoring the switch of housing benefit to the social security programme). Both current expenditure (mainly subsidies to local authority housing revenue accounts) and capital expenditure (such as building new houses) are way below their levels of 1978/9. The fall in current spending has had its impact lessened by the fact that half of the cut has turned up again as housing benefit in the social security budget.

Taken together, current housing expenditure and housing benefits (including the rents of those on SB) have been roughly constant in real terms since 1976 – what has changed is the balance between them.[5] The fall in capital spending has been unmoderated, however, and has led to a huge decline in public sector housebuilding – down from 84,000 housing starts in 1979 to 36,000 in 1985. It should be remembered, though, that the cuts began in 1976 – 1979 housing starts were already less than half of the 180,000 achieved in 1975 and 1976.

At a time of rising homelessness and increasing pressure on local authority housing departments, the combination of the sale of a tenth of the local authority stock (by and large the best tenth) and the drying up of new building has had obvious implications for the choices available to the poor. This is one area where the government has succeeded in cutting expenditure, as well as in reducing the level of public services.

Public squalor

Housing is just one area where cut-backs in capital spending have reduced the stock of assets available to provide public services. The poor rely more on public services than do those enjoying the private affluence of rising real earnings for those in work and tax cuts for the richest. The neglect of the community's assets, therefore, represents a fall in a significant part of the standard of living and quality of life of the poor, and one which is not measured by differences between the increases in incomes and prices. The decline in public capital spending also has an important effect on perceptions of public services: even if there are as many nurses and teachers around as there used to be, the peeling paint on the hospital and classroom walls and woodwork inside and outside gives a striking impression of decline.

Figure 1: *Public sector investment 1975-85*

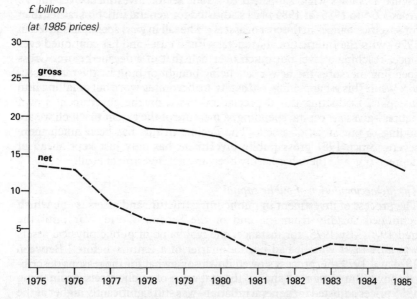

£ billion
(at 1985 prices)

Figure 2: *Public assets 1975-85*

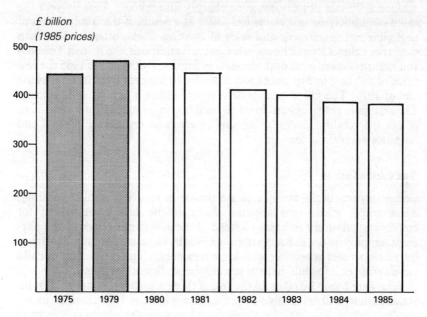

£ billion
(1985 prices)

Capital spending

Figure 1[6] shows what happened to public sector investment over the 10 years 1975 to 1985 (at 1985 prices adjusted for general inflation rather than for specific changes in the cost of assets). The fall in *gross* spending started in 1976 – with the International Monetary Fund cuts – and has continued ever since, reaching a level not much over half that of a decade before. Gross spending measures the new assets being bought or built by the public sector. While this is happening, old assets are becoming worn out or falling into disrepair. Deducting this depreciation – based on the government's own figures – gives *net* capital spending, a measure of the extent to which we are adding to our stock of assets. The decline in this has been much more severe. Since 1981 gross public investment has only just kept ahead of depreciation and there has hardly been any net investment at all.

The (de)accumulation of public capital

The process of investment in public infrastructure and assets is one which continued steadily from the end of the Second World War until the mid-1970s. By 1975, for instance, the real value of public physical assets was *three times* what it had been a quarter of a century before.[7] Between 1974 and 1979 this process slowed down somewhat for the reasons described above. But as figure 2 shows, the real value of public assets (again using 1985 prices adjusted for general inflation) was still significantly higher at the end than at the beginning.

Since 1979 this process has gone sharply into reverse. Year by year the value of publicly owned assets has *fallen* as a result of the combination of negligible net investment and sales of existing assets, often for less than their true value. Council house sales and privatisations like British Telecom and British Gas are some of the biggest examples. By the end of 1985 the real value of publicly owned assets had fallen by 20 per cent from its level at the end of 1979. The fall was equivalent to *£15 billion a year* (at 1985 prices). The results in terms of run-down council housing estates, water treatment plants that pollute rivers, collapsing sewers and crumbling schools and hospitals are plain to see.

Tax expenditures[8]

Certain aspects of the tax system are similar in nature to public spending. An example taken into account above is the new arrangement for employers' statutory sick pay – instead of the government making the payment, employers do, reducing their tax bills by the same amount. Mortgage interest tax relief is another well-known example. The conversion of child tax allowances into child benefit has also been allowed for above.

Great care has to be taken in the use of these measures, however. For instance, there will be double-counting if we look at *both* changes in tax burdens taking account of tax reliefs *and* include the reliefs as a form of

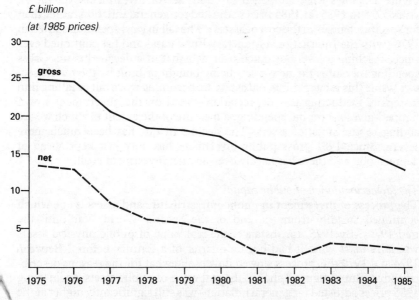

Figure 1: *Public sector investment 1975-85*

£ billion
(at 1985 prices)

gross

net

1975 1976 1977 1978 1979 1980 1981 1982 1983 1984 1985

Figure 2: *Public assets 1975-85*

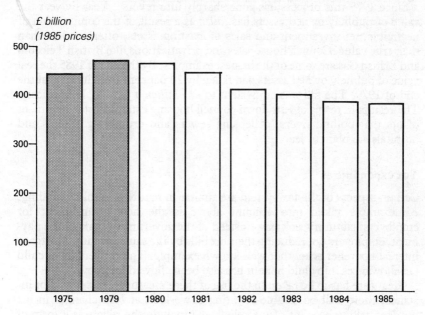

£ billion
(1985 prices)

1975 1979 1980 1981 1982 1983 1984 1985

Capital spending
Figure 1[6] shows what happened to public sector investment over the 10 years 1975 to 1985 (at 1985 prices adjusted for general inflation rather than for specific changes in the cost of assets). The fall in *gross* spending started in 1976 – with the International Monetary Fund cuts – and has continued ever since, reaching a level not much over half that of a decade before. Gross spending measures the new assets being bought or built by the public sector. While this is happening, old assets are becoming worn out or falling into disrepair. Deducting this depreciation – based on the government's own figures – gives *net* capital spending, a measure of the extent to which we are adding to our stock of assets. The decline in this has been much more severe. Since 1981 gross public investment has only just kept ahead of depreciation and there has hardly been any net investment at all.

The (de)accumulation of public capital
The process of investment in public infrastructure and assets is one which continued steadily from the end of the Second World War until the mid-1970s. By 1975, for instance, the real value of public physical assets was *three times* what it had been a quarter of a century before.[7] Between 1974 and 1979 this process slowed down somewhat for the reasons described above. But as figure 2 shows, the real value of public assets (again using 1985 prices adjusted for general inflation) was still significantly higher at the end than at the beginning.

Since 1979 this process has gone sharply into reverse. Year by year the value of publicly owned assets has *fallen* as a result of the combination of negligible net investment and sales of existing assets, often for less than their true value. Council house sales and privatisations like British Telecom and British Gas are some of the biggest examples. By the end of 1985 the real value of publicly owned assets had fallen by 20 per cent from its level at the end of 1979. The fall was equivalent to *£15 billion a year* (at 1985 prices). The results in terms of run-down council housing estates, water treatment plants that pollute rivers, collapsing sewers and crumbling schools and hospitals are plain to see.

Tax expenditures[8]

Certain aspects of the tax system are similar in nature to public spending. An example taken into account above is the new arrangement for employers' statutory sick pay – instead of the government making the payment, employers do, reducing their tax bills by the same amount. Mortgage interest tax relief is another well-known example. The conversion of child tax allowances into child benefit has also been allowed for above.

Great care has to be taken in the use of these measures, however. For instance, there will be double-counting if we look at *both* changes in tax burdens taking account of tax reliefs *and* include the reliefs as a form of

98

spending. The recent rapid rise in the value of reliefs has undoubtedly benefited the better off (see chapter 4), but it would be wrong to claim its effects twice. Secondly, the value of the reliefs shown in government publications often overstates what could be sensibly extracted by tightening them up. The personal allowances for income tax are a form of relief, but they are necessary to make the tax system progressive. The massive figures often quoted for the value of pension reliefs do not take account of the fact that regular pensions in payment are taxable – unlike, for instance, withdrawals from other forms of saving, such as building society accounts. Even mortgage interest tax relief is not necessarily a very good guide to the true tax advantages of owner-occupiers.

Nonetheless, the figures for tax reliefs do reveal some important trends. A further factor in the decline of unemployment benefit was that it became taxable in 1982, removing a relief which had been worth £200 million (at 1986/7 prices) in 1978/9. The yield from taxing benefits to the unemployed has been about £400m a year. With the age allowances for income tax losing ground against other personal allowances, their value fell to £430 million in 1986/7 – 16 per cent lower in real terms than in 1978/9, a slightly larger fall than would be caused simply by the cut in the basic rate. Meanwhile, the value of relief on life assurance premiums was, at £570 million, some 13 per cent higher in real terms, despite the abolition of relief on *new* policies in the 1984 budget. But perhaps most notably, the value of mortgage interest tax relief had risen to £4,500 million by 1986/7, more than twice its real level of eight years before, despite the cut in the basic rate of tax. *The increase in the real cost of mortgage interest tax relief over the period – £2.4 billion at 1986/7 prices – was the same size as the real fall in net public capital spending on housing.*

Conclusions

Looking through the public spending programme in this way gives the clue to understanding the paradox of rising public spending at a time of cuts. As certain areas of spending have been cut, so others have risen in response. As the cuts in the building programme for new housing have proceeded, the costs of SB for unemployed construction workers and claimants forced to live in board and lodging have risen. As cuts in current subsidies to local authority tenants have driven up rents, so the cost of housing benefit has risen. As the wider effects of the 1979-81 deflation spread through the economy, so the costs of unemployment to the social security budget rose. The government certainly tried to keep down spending, and in many cases succeeded in reducing real spending per beneficiary, but it could not stop it growing overall, partly because its own policies were creating new and increased demands.

The rising costs of the social security programme reflect no more than the impact of the increasing numbers of pensioners, unemployed people and people living in poverty. They mask the impact of the successive cuts that have been made in the social security programme. The House of Commons Library has estimated that these cuts were running at nearly £3 billion a year by 1986/7, a cumulative total of over £11 billion since 1979. This extra spending has been insufficient to keep up the living standards of those already dependent on benefits with the country's rising prosperity as a whole. It has done little to moderate the losses of those newly dependent on benefits through unemployment. Although the government has not yet succeeded in dismantling the welfare state, it can take no credit for the way in which spending on the welfare state has risen in response to growing poverty and inequality. It has, after all, spent a considerable amount of effort in attempting to restrain that response. Eight years on, it is clear that, contrary to the government's belief, *attempts to cut* public expenditure lie at the heart of Britain's present economic difficulties.

CHAPTER 11

Reforming social security – despite the claimant

Carol Walker

It was not to be expected that one of the major achievements of two terms of Thatcher government would be to place social security high on the political agenda. The plans set out in the 1979 Conservative Party Manifesto seemed to do no more than repeat some well worn objectives: to simplify the social security system, to restore the incentive to work, to reduce the poverty trap and to bring more help to those in need. With hindsight, they provided a forewarning of significant policy changes.

In the first Thatcher administration many of the fundamental principles on which social security policy had been founded since 1948 were challenged. This laid the foundation for the more fundamental attack on the benefits structure and benefits claimants which was to follow in the second administration. In *Thatcherism and the poor*, the authors summarised the government's early initiatives in social security. It is appropriate here to reflect on those changes and analyse their impact on developments during the second term, which are discussed in chapters 12 and 13.

What is wrong with social security? A view from the right

Two major themes have dominated government discussion and action on social security. First, it costs too much. Secondly, claimants have on occasions been presented not as victims of the current social and economic climate but in much more cynical terms – at worst, as being fraudulent or 'abusing' the system; at best, as not being 'genuinely' poor.

The 'millstone' theory of social security
A cumulative total of over £11 billion has been cut from the social security budget since 1979.[1] The process began with the package of proposals which culminated in the first Social Security Act 1980. This package, Patrick Jenkin, then secretary of state for social services, told the House of Commons, 'faces up to some of the problems confronting the nation from the rising share of the national income absorbed by social security'.[2] It heralded the first cuts in the social security programme by breaking the link between

101

the uprating of long-term benefits and increases in earnings. The standard of living of those dependent on state benefits was to be allowed to fall even further behind the earnings of those in work.

Further cuts were introduced in the Social Security (No 2) Act 1980. These included the abolition of earnings related supplement (ERS) and 'temporary' cuts in the level of invalidity benefit and unemployment and other short-term benefits. At the same time, an administrative sleight of hand resulted in steady cuts in the real value of the national insurance children's additions and the eventual abolition of those paid with short-term benefits. Several major initiatives were taken in the field of benefits: the 1980 reform of the supplementary benefit (SB) scheme (taken over from the previous Labour government), the introduction of housing benefit (HB) and, later, the introduction of the Fowler reforms. All these have been done on, at best, a nil-cost basis – because of the allegedly crippling cost of the social security system.

Despite being given a nil-cost remit, both the early SB reforms and the introduction of HB were presented as offering greater legal rights and administrative advantages for claimants. By the second term of office, the government saw less need to emphasise any advantages for claimants. Other goals were more important.

The Green Paper on the Reform of Social Security[3] is littered with references to the size of the social security budget. The stated objective of targeting help on those in greatest need has to be understood in that context. In the Green Paper, one of the three main objectives identified is that

> the social security system must be consistent with the overall objectives for the economy . . . Social security . . . is responsible for a major share of the current heavy tax burden on individuals and companies . . . continued growth of this burden could severely damage the prospects for economic growth.[4]

The argument is clear: social security costs too much: therefore claimants, or some groups of claimants, will have to manage on less. The government has put into practice its stated objective of ending the 'absolute priority [of social security spending] over spending on defence, the police, hospitals or schools – or over the need for proper control of public spending as a whole'.[5] Neither the Green Paper nor the White Paper discusses the adequacy of benefits; neither addresses the question of whether claimants can survive on current or, in many cases, even lower levels of support.

From victims to being victimised

'We have clamped down firmly on fraud and abuse of social security.'[6] This is one of the achievements listed in a 200-word section on social security in the 1983 Conservative Manifesto. Certainly, the government has been assiduous in its work in this area. Whilst few would argue with the principle that social security should go only to those who are legally eligible, many find the justification (made by Labour and Conservative governments alike) that crackdowns on 'fraud and abuse' create 'an atmosphere . . . in which "honest" people will feel more able to claim' unconvincing. More realistic is the assumption that 'myths about widespread fraud deter people from applying for benefits, because all claimants are tarred with the same brush and the stigma of claiming is intensified'.[7]

But such was the importance attached to this alleged problem that the DHSS was allowed to recruit over 1,000 additional staff to intensify the crackdown on fraud activity at a time when strikes were occurring in local offices because of understaffing in benefit administration (see chapter 12).[8] 1980 also saw the introduction of Specialists Claims Control teams in some regional offices to seek out specific types of fraud. In 1983, Regional Benefit Investigation Teams (RBITs) were established.[9]

A recurring theme over the past eight years has been what the prime minister, amongst others, has liked to call 'the why work syndrome'. Even though the former Supplementary Benefits Commission (SBC), the civil servants reviewing the SB scheme in 1978 and, most recently, the DHSS cohort study of the unemployed, amongst others, have concluded that social security's disincentive effect has been exaggerated, the government has put considerable emphasis on policies to ensure that those registered as unemployed are indeed looking for work, and willing and able to take a job if offered (see chapter 8). In addition, the disqualification period for 'voluntary' unemployment has been doubled, thus further discouraging people from giving up jobs.

The benefits system itself has provided additional financial incentive to get people off benefit – if any were needed – by continuing to discriminate against the unemployed. The exclusion of the long-term unemployed from the higher rate of SB is a long standing and widely recognised iniquity, for which the last Labour government must take considerable responsibility. It is shameful at a time when there are well over one million people registered as unemployed who have been drawing benefit for over one year.

In addition, there have been several cuts in benefit justified by the disincentive argument. For instance, ERS was scrapped in 1982, according to Patrick Jenkin, because it 'does add to income out of work and therefore at the margin does not encourage the return to work'.[10] This philosophy was reiterated in Fowler's Green Paper:

> While it is one of the functions of the social security system to help those who are unemployed, it is self-defeating if it creates barriers to the creation of jobs, to job mobility or to people rejoining the labour force. Clearly such obstacles exist if people believe themselves better off out of work than in work.[11]

As Fran Bennett shows (in chapter 13), many cuts in social security provision made in the 1986 Social Security Act were justified by downgrading the help available to those on benefit, to the lower level of support given to low wage earners. Equality of treatment, but equality of injustice, equality of poverty. As is shown in chapter 13 also, many of the cuts and changes in benefits which have taken place or are in the pipeline have actually worsened the 'poverty trap'.

Blaming the victim

The zeal with which the DHSS has pursued fraud and abuse over the past eight years has been questioned on a number of grounds. First, as discussed above, because of its adverse impact on 'genuine' claimants and potential claimants.

Secondly, there is its impact on public opinion. In the past, governments have been quick to respond to press and public criticism of fraud or abuse of the social security system. But in recent years, it is the government itself which has helped to orchestrate the issue. Can it be a coincidence that a government committed to cutting social security expenditure has put so much effort and resources into publicising the alleged dishonesty of claimants? By helping to foster a hostile attitude towards benefit recipients, a general climate is created which accepts cuts in benefit provision. Thus, claimants become increasingly marginalised from the rest of the community, not only because of their low income but also because of their lack of status and public support.

A third concern stems from a change in DHSS policy away from an emphasis on prosecution as an indicator of the success of anti-fraud work to the amount of benefit 'saved' by 'fraudulent' claimants ceasing to claim or repaying 'overpaid' benefit. The dubious nature of the 'savings' produced have been discussed elsewhere.[12]

The Lord Chief Justice, Lord Lane, has noted the change of policy in the DHSS away from prosecuting alleged offenders and, instead, issuing warnings and 'encouraging' claimants to cease drawing benefit. Between 1980 and 1982, the number of prosecutions dropped from 30,000 to 13,000. While fewer prosecutions of social security claimants is welcome at one level (especially when the much lower prosecution rate of tax fraud is taken into account),[13] concern has arisen that claimants' rights have been trampled on in the process. Nowhere has the infringement of claimants rights been more apparent than in the 'Oxfraud' incident' (see chapter 2).[14]

In such cases, people may be driven off benefit by fear and pressure from officers rather than by proof of guilt. A survey of claimants in Leeds found that 'many respondents lived in fear of inadvertently doing wrong, or not reporting something which would later rebound on them'. One claimant said: 'You always think you're doing wrong . . . I think I'm doing wrong every time because I don't know what I can have. That thing [the fraud warning printed in red on order books] frightens you to death.'[15]

What's wrong with social security? The claimant's view

None of the above discussion of the government's concern for social security reflects any consideration or understanding of what it is like to be a social security claimant. Decisions are made for ideological, administrative or financial reasons, *despite* their impact on claimants.

In the Green Paper it is argued: 'The living standards of those most dependent on social security benefits can . . . be seen to have improved substantially over the post-war period and in this respect a prime objective of the social security system has been achieved.'[16] Such a statement is made in the context of rejecting a relative standard of poverty (see chapter 1). It also illustrates the complacency of the government regarding the level of benefit. Cuts in the benefit system have frequently been defended on the grounds that 'the poorest' – those on SB – are being protected. There was no attempt in the Green Paper to consider the adequacy of that protection, let alone the circumstances of those just above SB level who have suffered some of the most severe cuts. Yet there is a wealth of information to show the difficulty that claimants have in living on state benefits. The Green Paper refers to none of this.

There have been numerous independent and DHSS-sponsored research projects, one aspect of which has been to examine the living standards of those on benefits. A national study conducted by the Policy Studies Institute (PSI) looked at the operation of the 1980 SB reforms.[17] One claimant in six reported that they were 'getting into difficulties'. This ranged from one in 20 pensioners to one in two couples with children.

In another study looking at the impact of the new scheme, over three-quarters of supplementary allowance recipients said their benefit was not enough to meet their day-to-day expenses. Half the pensioner respondents said their money was not enough. Even amongst those who said they did have enough, their comments often reflected resignation and a feeling of gratitude for receiving anything, rather than a comfortable standard of living. One pensioner said: 'I'd like better food, but [I] can't complain. I don't need as much food now that I'm older. I can't complain . . . but I'm waiting for the pension all the time. I manage, but only just.' One lone parent qualified her view that SB was *adequate* with the statement: 'But then, I've always had to do without – new clothes, empty cupboards, being able to go out.'[18]

In the PSI study, half the couples with children said they ran out of money before the next payday *most weeks*; 68 per cent of claimants reported that they had had to find money over and above their weekly benefit in the previous 12 months, and about one-third had used part or all of their savings. Since pensioners were the group most likely to have any savings, younger people had to find other ways of bridging the gap between income and expenditure – the only solutions were to incur debt or to do without.

A recent report by the London Food Commission found that people on

105

low incomes face serious food problems.[19] Food was a 'flexible' item in the household budget, which tended to get cut back when money was short. Burghes found that four-fifths of the 65 families studied often missed meals because they could not afford them.[20] A special report in *Woman* magazine concluded:

> Poverty is one of the main reasons for malnutrition, because when parents become unemployed, one of the first areas of expense to be reduced is food ... Various recent studies have shown that it is impossible to eat a balanced diet and pay for all other basic essentials such as home, heating and clothing ... Among the families ... was one where ... the kitchen was padlocked at night to stop the children getting to the food.[21]

Edwina Currie has attempted to blame poor people for their poor diets, but it has been calculated that the recommended National Advisory Committee on Nutrition Education (NACNE) diet costs 35 per cent more than the typical diet of a low income family. Many other independent studies have argued that the SB scale rates are not sufficient to meet a family's needs.[22] SSAC, the government's advisory body on social security, has also supported this view.

The government's response has been to argue for more effective 'targeting'. The reforms in the pipeline continue the now well-established practice of shifting resources within the social security budget: from those with 'less' needs – now defined as non-householders, the elderly, the young, and those without children – to those in 'greatest need' – families with children (see chapter 13). The case for giving more help to the latter group may be obvious; that the former can afford to provide the money for this improvement is far more doubtful. *The fact that it is clear that families with children are not getting enough does not mean that other not-so-poor groups are getting too much.* Unfortunately, that corollary is implicit in the present government's approach to social security.

From legal rights to a legal right to nothing

Despite the increased reliance on means-tested benefits, the Fowler reforms totally neglect the issue of take-up of benefit and fail to give proper consideration to how the major changes will actually affect claimants. Take-up of entitlement, far from being regarded as a sign of policy success, has been a cause for concern, and then a justification for cutting back.

The 1980 SB changes were presented as having advantages for claimants – even for those who ended up with less money. Then, the government recommended the new legal framework of the scheme on the grounds that it would give claimants more rights, which would be easier for them to be informed about, to understand and to claim.

Between 1980 and 1985 the number of single payments grew rapidly, from 1.1 million to 4.1 million (even though payments for clothing and footwear, which had accounted for over half the lump-sum payments before 1980, had been severely curtailed). This increase could not be explained by the rise in claimants over the period. The rate per 1,000 claimants increased by nearly 2½ times over the same period. A great government success for the objective set out in the White Paper on the 1980 reforms that 'all claimants will reap the benefits of the emphasis on legal entitlement and published rules, and on simplification'?[23] No. The government was surprised, even shocked, at its own success.

The hollowness of the government's commitment to legal rights was shown when this larger than expected take-up, which as SSAC pointed out occurred despite lack of government publicity,[24] was met with severe cutbacks in the availability of single payments in 1986 (see chapter 12). In the longer term, the government is making yet another attempt to cut the costs of single payments expenditure (which was the hidden goal of the regulation based system) by abolishing most of them, and instead setting up the social fund, which is to be primarily a cash-limited loans scheme (see chapter 13).

Housing benefit might be seen as a similar 'success'. It now reaches one in three households. Is the government proud of a system that helps so many poor households? On the contrary, the Green Paper warns against 'constructing systems, such as we now have in housing benefit which grow from schemes designed to give help to those most in need until they cover much wider areas of the population. We must target the resources we have more effectively.'[25] The government does not, however, make a similar and consistent demand of mortgage interest tax relief.

The administration of benefits: creating a buffer zone

Decentralisation
As the benefits system itself has been modified to be less responsive to client needs, so the administration has become less client-centred and increasingly is moving away from the DHSS.

The DHSS's first disengagement from benefits administration came with the introduction of HB. The responsibility for paying all rent and rate rebates was passed over to the local authorities, despite in very many cases an unpreparedness for the task. The local authorities accepted this role as a way of reducing their arrears. The government agreed to pay their administrative costs, though this is now being threatened by the new arrangements laid down in the Social Security Act 1986.

The introduction of HB proved to be a catastrophe for claimants. There were major delays in payment and massive errors in administration. It also represented a major blow to claimants' dignity and independence. Local authority tenants lost the right to be responsible for paying their rent.

An advantage for claimants was that sometimes local authorities used the discretion available to them to pay more generous rebates. These discretionary powers, together with local authorities' rights to provide free school meals to low income families not covered by the legislation, will be removed under the Social Security Act 1986. The government is requiring local authorities to take over administration, thereby enabling it to show a reduction in the number of civil servants, but is taking away any discretion local authorities have in the level and scope of benefits provided.

Privatisation
The government has moved towards privatisation of the benefits system in two ways. Employers are increasingly being involved. In 1983 employers took over responsibility for statutory sick pay (SSP), to be paid for the first eight weeks of sickness in place of sickness benefit. In April 1986 that period was extended to 28 weeks. A recent report has chronicled the problems which this move has created for people going sick.[26] Nevertheless, in April 1987 the government introduced statutory maternity pay to replace maternity benefits and maternity pay. An attempt to make employers responsible for the new family credit scheme (the successor to FIS) was only dropped after considerable pressure (see chapter 13).

The transfer of administration from the DHSS to employers, and the local authorities, has enabled the DHSS to cut its administrative costs and staffing (though such savings are illusory because local authorities have to employ people to do the work and employers are reimbursed via their national insurance contributions). Such changes also place an intermediary between the claimant and the state. An employee may be much less inclined to pursue problems over SSP with the employer. In addition, blame for problems with this provision may fall on the employer or the local authority rather than on central government, where responsibility does and should lie.

In the area of pensions, the government is subsidising the private sector to make it profitable for them to provide private pensions, as an alternative to making comprehensive and adequate state provision (see chapter 12).

Do-it-yourself social security
A more pervasive and invidious method of privatising administration has been the transfer of responsibility from the benefits system to claimants themselves. In order to cut staff, new administrative procedures have been introduced which place more onus on claimants to identify their own needs, to find out about help which might be available, to obtain any appropriate forms and to fill them in correctly. The introduction of postal claiming and the policy of radically reducing the number of home visits, means that there are fewer opportunities through the formal administration for claimants' needs to be identified and met. There would be an outcry if fraud investigations were conducted by post. Should expectations be lower and investigations less thorough when the DHSS is pursuing what should be its primary role, of getting benefits to those who are entitled to them?

The state system is also providing less help to fewer people. Many young people, students and others whose incomes take them just over the SB level have been removed completely from eligibility for some benefits. In reforming the SB scheme in 1980, the government put some of the most common and pressing needs which poor families have, most importantly replacement clothing, outside the scope of the scheme. The income support scheme and the social fund will put many other needs outside their remit. It will be claimants who will carry the cost of that loss.

Conclusion

As David Piachaud has illustrated (see chapter 3) the number of people dependent on state benefits has risen sharply since 1979. Claimants themselves are now having to pay the price for the growing number of people dependent on the state which has led to the increase in social security spending (see chapter 10). They are, in other words, being asked to pay twice: first with the loss of work and then through less generous benefits and an increasingly punitive benefits system. It is a classic example of individualising the problem, ignoring wider social conditions and 'blaming the victim' for his or her own misfortune.

Despite public protestations that its social security policies do protect the poor and are sensitive to their needs, there is little practical evidence of this. The 'genuinely poor' are being narrowed down in a similar way to the 'genuinely' unemployed. More and more people are falling *outside* the government's restricted definition of those in need.

The government has been largely immune to criticism and shown very little willingness to take on board outside views, except at the margins of policy. Despite a united and vociferous opposition to the Social Security Act 1986, very few concessions were made even after a string of defeats in the House of Lords. Even SSAC has expressed concern that it is being bypassed on some important issues. In its 1986/87 Report it expressed concern 'at the unusual use of primary legislation to extend the period of reduction of supplementary benefit for voluntary unemployment when this could have been achieved by regulations. We were assured that this had not been done in order to bypass the Committee . . . Nevertheless, we regret the introduction of these changes'.[27] A similar anxiety was expressed when the government wanted to extend the 'quarantine' period (under which regulations made soon after the passing of legislation are not referred to SSAC). No regulations laid within 12 months of the 1986 Act have to be so referred.

The government has been increasingly cavalier about the views of claimants, pressure groups and its own advisory committee on the impact of its changes on claimants. But this is symptomatic of the major problem which is that claimants have effectively been disenfranchised; their needs have been ignored; they have been marginalised, and in too many cases forgotten. Only by adopting such a posture, can the government tell the poor that they will have to wait, while the affluent are allowed to become still more affluent.

CHAPTER 12

The bottom line: has Conservative social security protected the poor?

Peter Esam

The approach to social security under Margaret Thatcher's leadership has been characterised by an attack on the principle of universal state provision. Vigorous efforts have been made by the Conservatives to reduce the role of the state in favour of private provision. Within the state sector itself the major means-tested schemes – supplementary benefit and housing benefit – have been developed to take on a permanent mass role, while non-means-tested benefits have been pushed into the background. In many parts of the state sector a process of 'active erosion' has been encouraged: cuts in the relative value of benefits and local administrative collapses have tended to discredit the idea of state provision itself, and so paved the way for further privatisation.

The Conservative period of office has seen massive increases in the number of unemployed people and one-parent families dependent on benefits. No attempt has been made to tailor the system of insurance benefits to meet these needs. Indeed, between 1978 and 1984 the number of unemployed people on the means-tested SB rose by more than 50 per cent. The government has decided that the needs of these additional claimants should be catered for through the system of means-tested benefits.

At the same time, the government has defended the cuts which have been made in social security by arguing that the poorest have been protected. The validity of this defence – and of the whole policy – depends crucially on two questions. First, have the main means-tested benefits provided adequate protection for the poor over the last eight years? Secondly, have those groups who are particularly vulnerable to poverty – such as the elderly, families with children, ethnic minorities and people with disabilities – been protected from the effects of the social security cuts? In this chapter we consider the government's record in each of these areas.

Supplementary benefits[1]

The value of the safety net

The government has made much of the fact that since 1979 SB rates have kept ahead of price inflation. But this is a misleading comparison. Price inflation is higher for the poor than for the rich, because the prices of goods they buy tend to rise faster. Between 1974 and 1982, for instance, inflation was 17 per cent higher for poor households than for rich ones. For this reason, a comparison between benefit rates and earnings is more helpful. Between 1979 and 1986 the value of the long-term rate of SB for a couple fell by nearly 5 per cent relative to average net income – from 45 per cent to 40.3 per cent.[2]

The 1980 changes to the SB scheme, in particular, were designed to offer greater legal rights. However, legal entitlement is of little practical value unless claimants actually gain access to benefits. This is of particular importance in a scheme such as SB, which is intended to provide primary protection against poverty. Yet the take-up of SB has always been problematic. And, in addition, there has been an effective break-down of administration in some parts of the country. In inner London it is now common for claimants to wait months – sometimes over a year – to get decisions on claims for grants and weekly additions. Offices are frequently closed to the public, and when they are open there are long waits for interviews. Telephone access is often almost impossible, especially for those reliant on public phones. Meanwhile, extra resources have been poured into anti-fraud work, producing an atmosphere of hostility and suspicion between staff and claimants.

'Rough justice'

In 1979 the Conservatives inherited an SB scheme which was supposed to meet individual need, with the amount of SB received depending not just on the level of the scale rate, but also on the 'extras' which could be claimed in the form of grants and weekly additions. Within 18 months of coming into office sweeping reforms had been implemented, based on a review carried out under the Labour government. The changes involved a large element of 'rough justice',[3] a term coined by the civil servants who drew up the original proposals on which the 1980 changes were based in the interests of adapting SB to a 'mass role' and restricting expenditure on the scheme. Entitlement to grants and additions was strictly defined in a plethora of regulations, and some needs previously met were excluded. In particular, clothing grants became extremely hard to obtain – a change which specially affected families with children.

Since 1980 the process of restricting entitlement to grants has continued unabated, tempered only by the occasional improvement. In many cases, the cuts have been relatively small. However, the Social Security Advisory Committee made the point in its latest annual report:

A particular proposal to reduce expenditure may be reasonable in itself, but when viewed in the light of cumulative changes it may be more stringent than at first appears. We must consider the total effect on

111

claimants of the many changes – beneficent as well as adverse – which are made to social security benefits over the years.[4]

In February 1986 the government announced drastic changes in the single payments regulations. 'Essential furniture and household equipment' was redefined so as to exclude floor-coverings, curtains, chairs, tables, storage units and many smaller items. The callousness of the new regulations is exemplified by the rules regarding bedding for children. Parents whose children lack sheets or blankets do not now qualify for a bedding grant unless they have just moved home under specified circumstances, or have increased the size of their family within the last four weeks. Evidence is already emerging of the hardship these cuts are creating.

These regulations, which came into force in August 1986, were plainly framed in anticipation of the planned abolition of single payments in April 1988 and the introduction of the Social Fund (see chapter 13). They are typical of the process of 'active erosion'. Once a form of provision such as the system of single payments has been seen to be failing in practice, it is much easier to argue for its complete abolition. Moreover, if it does occur, the moment of abolition will appear that much less significant because single payments have already been slashed. Inevitably, comparisons will be misleadingly made between the Social Fund and single payments as they now stand. Yet the current level of provision threatens to be nothing more than a transitional phase in the total abolition of single payments.

Heating

The past eight years have seen several changes in rules regarding heating additions, and these have particularly affected long-term beneficiaries of SB – people with disabilities, lone parents, carers and pensioners. Central heating additions have been abolished. In 1984 the government introduced a £1 deduction from weekly additions for special needs, applied to all those getting the long-term rate of SB. Previously, a 50 pence deduction had applied to some additions, but the new deduction applied even to heating – and many lost out as a result. On the other hand, the government has extended automatic entitlement to the higher rate heating addition to those aged over 85; and entitlement to the lower heating addition to those with young children, those over 65 and those entitled to the long-term rate of SB on health grounds. However, in the vast majority of cases these additions should have been in payment anyway. Unfortunately, these improvements must be viewed primarily as cosmetic changes.

The government's policy on exceptionally cold weather payments has been characterised by extraordinary zig-zags. Regulations introduced after a review of the system were jettisoned by ministers during the next spell of cold weather – in January 1987. The government claimed this change of heart as evidence of compassion. But many pensioners and others suffering from the cold must have questioned why protection from the cold should have to depend on ministers responding in an ad hoc way to public pressure.

112

Housing costs: 'the biggest fiasco'

Introducing housing benefit

The Times called the introduction of housing benefit (HB) in 1982/3 'the biggest fiasco in the history of the welfare state'. The new scheme involved transferring responsibility for meeting the housing costs of those on SB from the DHSS to local authorities. The government's determination to introduce the scheme at no extra cost resulted in absurd complexities – such as 'housing benefit supplement', incomprehensible to non-specialists. The scheme was introduced too quickly, so that neither the government nor local authorities were able to plan and control developments properly. The result was widespread administrative chaos.

Cuts

Housing benefit was introduced in the context of government policy which aimed at making council housing self-financing. Between 1979 and 1984 council house rents increased by an average of 40 per cent in real terms. The government argued that the poor would be protected from the effects of these increases by housing benefit. Yet even as HB was first introduced, the juggling of entitlement between claimants meant that some low-income tenants (and owners) lost substantially. The losers were mainly those with incomes above the HB needs allowance, and those with non-dependants (ie, someone other than a dependent child) living at home. 'Transitional protection' was available to soften the impact of the cuts on existing claimants. But, with extraordinary insensitivity, the government announced cuts in HB expenditure of £230 million before this transitional protection had even run out. Moreover, this second round of cuts was aimed primarily at the same groups which had suffered first time around.

In its White Paper on Public Expenditure, the government justified these cuts as designed 'to concentrate resources on those most in need of help'. It is hard to see how the government could really hope to achieve this objective by taking money out of a scheme designed to help the poor. Moreover, the announcement of these cuts (in 1983) followed an announcement earlier in the same year which increased the size of mortgage on which tax relief can be claimed – an expensive measure which primarily benefits the better-off.

Under the HB scheme, benefit is reduced by a certain percentage of any income which the claimant has in excess of his or her 'needs allowance'. This percentage reduction is known as a 'taper'. Increases in tapers particularly hit those in low paid work, and those on non-means-tested state benefits such as retirement and invalidity pensions. Table 1 shows how the tapers have been increased since HB was introduced.

Increases in the amount of money deducted from the rebate where there is a non-dependant living in the household have also been dramatic. A claimant who has a working daughter or son living at home now loses £10.85 per week from HB, compared to £5.90 in November 1982. The government's

Table 1:
Changes in HB tapers 1982-7

	April 1982	April 1983	April 1984	Nov 1984	Nov 1985	April 1987
Rates	6%	7%	9%	9%	13%	13%
Rent	17%	21%	26%	29%	29%	33%
Total	23%	28%	35%	38%	42%	46%

own Social Security Advisory Committee has remarked how the focus of these cuts seems to run counter to the government's professed objective of improving work incentives. They have substantially worsened the 'poverty trap'. The dismal conclusion is that the desire to save public expenditure at the expense of the poor has overridden all other considerations.

The setting up of an independent review of the HB scheme within a year of its launch did not herald a more consistent or compassionate approach. On the contrary, around £450 million of HB cuts are planned under the Social Security Act 1986 (see chapter 13). The government's decision to cut assistance with mortgage interest repayments during the first four months on SB was equally inconsistent with its normal stance of support for owner- occupation, and will lead to still further anxiety and debt for the newly unemployed.

Moving-on the homeless

The homeless have been pursued assiduously as part of the government's determination to reduce benefits expenditure. Under the post-1980 regulations, the homeless could claim for board and lodging charges up to a cash ceiling. These were set by DHSS adjudication officers in the light of local charges. Under this system the government could not exert direct control over the number of people who claimed, or over the level of local ceilings. Moreover, government restrictions on local authority spending on both ordinary housing and on special provision for the elderly and handicapped have ensured a large increase in demand for bed and breakfast accommodation, hostels and places in private homes of all sorts.

The whole area demands a coordinated policy, which takes into account housing need, the provision of support for care in the community and adequate benefit provision. Yet the government's response to these problems has been confined to numerous attempts to limit benefit provision. In September 1984, the government announced regulations to freeze local ceilings on board and lodging payments which were subsequently declared unlawful. In April 1985 far more punitive arrangements were put forward. Despite further legal set-backs, the government eventually succeeded in making these arrangements stick. The locally determined ceilings were replaced by regional limits set by the secretary of state, and young people (under the age of 26) were only allowed to claim ordinary board and lodging payments for a limited period – between two and eight weeks. Rather than move from area to area as itinerants, many young people have been forced to sleep rough on the streets. The full social cost of this draconian measure is hard to estimate.

National insurance and retirement

A government only weakly committed to the idea of universal state provision was likely to act quickly to cut back the system of insurance related benefits. The two Social Security Acts introduced in 1980 hit hardest at national insurance benefits: changing the method of uprating pensions and other long-term benefits; abolishing earnings-related benefits for 'short-term' benefits, and introducing a 'temporary' 5 per cent cut in the level of unemployment, sickness, maternity and invalidity benefits.

Pensioners lose out
The newly-elected government of 1979 declared its 'firm intention that pensioners can confidently look forward to sharing in the increased standards of living of the country as a whole'.[5] Yet one of its first actions was to reverse legislation which guaranteed pensioners that right.

Under the 1975 legislation, introduced with all-party support, retirement pensions and other long-term national insurance benefits were annually uprated in line with earnings or prices – whichever was higher. The Social Security Act 1980 changed this requirement, so that pensions need only be uprated in line with prices, which usually rise more slowly than earnings. Had the government continued to uprate pensions in line with earnings the pension for a couple would now be more than £11.30 per week higher than it actually is.[6]

The unemployed lose out
Unemployment benefit has suffered under the Tories. Although the 5 per cent abatement made in 1980 was made good in 1983, after strong pressure from Conservative MPs, the earnings-related supplement and child dependancy additions no longer exist. These cuts have so reduced the role of unemployment benefit that by 1985/6 72 per cent of unemployed people claiming unemployment benefit had to have it topped up by means-tested SB.[7]

Since 1983 the unemployed have continued to fare badly. The government has ignored the repeated advice of its own Social Security Advisory Committee that the long-term rate of SB should be extended to the unemployed. Instead of improving provision for the unemployed during a period of mass involuntary unemployment, the government's programme has focussed on massaging the employment statistics by restricting the access of the unemployed to those benefits which do exist for them. The maximum period of disqualification from unemployment benefit has been more than doubled, and procedures for vetting availability for work have been considerably tightened (see chapter 8).

Sickness and disability: shedding responsibility

The government has now managed to shed responsibility for the administration of benefit for short-term sickness. In April 1983 it introduced statutory sick pay (SSP) for the first eight weeks of sickness. Undeterred by evidence that the scheme was resulting in a high rate of error in payments to the sick, in April 1986 SSP was extended to cover the first 28 weeks of sickness. For that whole period a claimant with earnings under £76.50 per week now gets just £32.85 SSP, even if s/he is the sole earner in a couple. Under the rules as they stood at 1979, s/he would now be receiving £48.65 sickness benefit, plus earnings-related supplement, plus additions for any children. SSP is also subject to tax and national insurance payments, unlike sickness benefit.

The long-term sick have been treated slightly better under the Conservatives second term than they were first time around. In November 1983 the 'invalidity trap' was removed. This anomaly had meant that some recipients of invalidity benefit were ineligible for SB, even though their incomes were below the level of the long-term rate of SB. Two years later the 5 per cent cut in invalidity benefit was finally restored – five years after its imposition. However, this good news was off-set by a major cut which had the political advantage to the government of being much harder to understand. From November 1985 the chronically sick have only been able to receive *either* the invalidity allowance (an extra allowance related to the age when the claimant first falls sick), *or* the additional pension (an earnings-related addition). Previously, it was possible to receive both, and indeed there is no logical reason for off-setting one against the other. This can mean a reduction in benefit entitlement of up to £8.30 per week.

Another cause of concern is the 1986 round of cuts in the industrial injuries scheme. Those suffering accidents at work are no longer entitled to a lump-sum disablement pension. The claimant now normally receives no compensation at all for 'minor' injuries, such as losing part of an index finger.

Women and social security

Disability benefits

Some of the most important developments in the field of benefits for disability and chronic sickness have been linked to moves to reduce direct discrimination against women, often necessitated by the provisions of the EEC's directive on equal treatment.[8] At long last, in November 1984 the notorious 'household duties test' was abolished. This test had meant that married women who claimed non-contributory invalidity pension (NCIP) had to prove that they were incapable of performing housework, as well as

116

passing the normal test of incapacity for paid work. However, the welcome for the removal of this degrading piece of discrimination was tempered by the government's decision to abolish NCIP itself along with the household duties test.

The benefit which replaced NCIP – severe disablement allowance – operates on a very restrictive test of severe disability. Whereas NCIP was payable after six months of sickness, the chronically sick claimant is only eligible for severe disablement allowance if s/he has been more or less continuously sick since before the age of 20. Eligibility has been so rigidly curtailed that in practice many married women who previously fell foul of the household duties test are still excluded.

On 23 June 1986 Norman Fowler grudgingly gave in to the force of the law, and announced that married women would no longer be prevented from claiming invalid care allowance. The EEC's Advocate General had already advised that the ban was unlawful. It was widely assumed that the European court would make a ruling to that effect on the following day, so Norman Fowler's announcement was just in time to save himself from the embarrassment of having his actions ruled unlawful again. However, there was widespread relief that he did not follow his own precedent, set in the case of NCIP, and simply abolish invalid care allowance.

Equal treatment? Women and supplementary benefit
The EEC directive has also brought about changes in the SB system. Under the directive, it would have been illegal to continue the rule barring married women from claiming SB. However, the equal treatment rules introduced in November 1983 contrived to comply with the letter of the law while making the minimum possible change to the structure of SB. Moreover, they did so in such a complex fashion that even experts confess difficulty in fathoming the rules. Under the new regulations, there still has to be one partner who makes a claim on behalf of a couple, and the selection is largely made on the basis of recent contact with the labour market: usually, it is still the man who ends up making the claim. (Further changes are, however, due under the 1986 Social Security Act.) Although the government has recently recognised the validity of the principle of financial privacy for women in tax matters, they have not been willing to consider applying the principle to social security.[9] The rules are based on the assumption that each family has one breadwinner, rather than the increasingly common pattern of dual income couples. (See also chapter 15).

Unequal treatment for ethnic minorities

The treatment of ethnic minority claimants has become considerably less equal during the two terms of the Conservative government (as was shown in chapter 7). The 1980 SB legislation made those who sponsor immigrants to enter the country liable for their financial support. In September 1984 an

117

immigration test was introduced into the housing benefit scheme, with rules excluding most categories of foreign students.

In December 1985 the DHSS issued a new circular on identification to local offices (S50/85). The circular rules out several forms of identification often relied on by ethnic minority claimants, and strongly advises against payments of benefit when there is a lack of evidence. Although some of these procedures were already applied in many local offices, the result has been to sanction and intensify the practice of demanding passports from ethnic minority claimants, and to justify frequent refusals of SB.

The survival of child benefit

As the government was forced to admit in its Green Paper: 'Child benefit is simple, well understood and popular.'[10] But it concluded that: 'Although the general principle of providing support to families through child benefit is important, the greatest priority for additional resources in the area of family support is to provide better targeted help for those on low incomes.' The evidence is that means-tested family support is, in fact, very badly targeted on poor families. Family income supplement (FIS), for example, reaches only 50 per cent of those eligible. The government's reluctance to accept the good sense of the public's positive verdict on child benefit is typical of its dogmatic distaste for any form of universal provision. However, it fortunately did not feel able to abolish the universal child benefit, despite strong rumours that this was planned under the 'Fowler' review. Instead, the government's grudging attitude to child benefit was revealed in its decision to uprate it by just 15 pence to £7.00 per week in November 1985. This represented a 5 per cent cut in its real value. The rate applying from April 1987 is still 35 pence short of its 1983 level (when a previous cut made in 1980 was restored). Under the Conservatives, the real value of child benefit has dropped, and there must be good grounds for fears that its value will not be restored and could be reduced still further under their stewardship.

Since 1980, the government has also systematically undermined the value of the child additions payable with national insurance benefits. The cash level of the additions for the 'short-term' benefits was progressively cut until, in November 1984, they were abolished altogether.

April 1987

Looking back over nearly eight years of Conservative government, it is apparent that the insurance system of benefits has been considerably undermined, to an extent that was to be expected, given the government's declared strategy. But it is also clear that the government has not succeeded in meeting its own standards for social security provision. The supplementary and housing benefit schemes have both failed badly. Although, overall,

118

SB rates have increased faster than the retail price index (although not faster than the low paid price index) a number of cuts have hurt the very poorest as well as dragging down some of those previously just above the poverty line. Benefits specially catering for vulnerable groups have also not escaped. Far from sharing in the fruits of increased prosperity, those not in paid employment have had to share out increased poverty.

In April 1987 Norman Fowler implemented the first major phase of the 1986 Social Security Act – the product of his various reviews. Following the experiment with statutory sick pay, the administration of maternity allowance is also to be privatised into the hands of employers. The result will be a loss of entitlement for women not employed during the year prior to their pregnancy. At the same time, both maternity grant and death grant are to be abolished. A classic example of 'active erosion': at £25 and £30 respectively, many consider their contribution so derisory that abolition was inevitable. As is dictated by the selectivist approach, the payments which replace them will be available to low income claimants only.

The founders of the modern welfare state boasted that social security provision for citizens would extend from 'the cradle to the grave'. Perhaps Norman Fowler is demonstrating an acute sense of history in his manner of implementing the first phase of his social security reviews: universal provision for the cradle and the grave is being abolished. Moreover, as if not satisfied to leave the symbolism there, the payments which are replacing the death and maternity grants are to be administered as part of the social fund – that new symbol of bureaucratic discretion distinguishing between the 'worthy' and the 'unworthy' poor.

CHAPTER 13

What future for social security?

Fran Bennett

The government's plans for social security in the near future are set out in the Social Security Act 1986. If the Conservatives are returned to power, the shape of the social security system is fairly clear already.

This chapter looks at the government's plans for changes in the social security system and analyses the likely impact of the main 'reforms' due to come into effect in April 1988. A more detailed analysis can be found in the guide to the Act produced by the Social Security Consortium.[1]

The reviews: aims and objectives

The reviews of pensions, housing benefit (HB), benefits for children and young people, and supplementary benefit (SB) were announced between November 1983 and April 1984. Maternity provision was to be examined separately by civil servants. A survey of disabled people was to be carried out, to assess their numbers and the severity of disabilities, before any review of benefits for disabled people was to take place. The report of the survey is due in 1988 (although disabled people will, of course, be affected by some of the changes to other benefits implemented in that year or before).

There were mixed motives behind the setting up of the four main reviews. While the pensions review may have been the most ideologically inspired, the HB review was the government's belated response to the widespread criticism of the introduction of the new scheme in 1982/3, and the chaos which ensued. The other two reviews, it was rumoured at the time, were promised by the DHSS as a 'quid pro quo' to the Treasury for having failed to deliver sufficient benefit cuts in previous years.[2]

Once the reviews had been set up, however, they had to be presented as a coherent exercise. In the Green Paper, published in June 1985, the government's aims were outlined as:

- encouraging self-reliance and independence;
- targeting resources on those who need them most;
- making the system simpler to understand and easier to administer;
- ensuring that the social security system was consistent with the government's overall economic objectives.[3]

Criticism and compromise

The government's proposals for change attracted considerable criticism. In fact, CPAG's analysis of 60 representative organisations' responses to the Green Paper found only two groups in overall agreement – the Institute of Directors and the Monday Club.[4] Norman Fowler's aim of 'carrying the great bulk of commonsense opinion with us'[5] was revealed as wishful thinking.

However, the White Paper published in December 1985, was – with the belated addition of figures to show the impact of the changes on various groups of people – largely unchanged from the Green Paper.[6] The only major change in policy was that the proposal to abolish completely the state earnings related pension scheme (SERPS) and make 'personal', private pensions compulsory – put forward amidst considerable controversy in the Green Paper – was dropped, and replaced by proposals to reduce SERPS entitlement and 'encourage' personal pensions instead. The other modification of significance was that the timing of most of the changes was altered from April 1987 to April 1988 (with the exception of those changes described in chapter 12). It was during the passage of the Social Security Bill through Parliament that, confronted by opposition from MPs and peers (often on an all-party basis), the government had to make some further modifications to its proposals.[7]

Proposals for change in 1988

Pensions

The government's proposals to change the shape of pension provision, by reducing entitlements under SERPS and encouraging more reliance on private pensions, broke with an all-party consensus on pensions that had been painfully built up in the 1970s. Opposition to the changes seemed to be anticipated by the government, as it repeatedly assured current pensioners that they would not lose out, and promised a 2 per cent payment of national insurance contributions to 'persuade' people to transfer from SERPS to personal pensions.

From 1999, entitlements under SERPS will start to be reduced. From April 2000, there will also be reductions in widows' and widowers' pensions. Overall, the changes will mean lower earnings-related pensions, in particular for the low paid, part-time workers and those who have a period of unemployment. The cost of SERPS will be halved over the next half century.

For those people who take out personal pensions – and for those whose employers change their pension schemes into money purchase arrangements (as they are allowed to under the Act) – there will be much greater uncertainty about the level of pension they will get. Far from ending the problem of having 'two nations' of pensioners, as Norman Fowler claimed he was doing, the changes will further divide pensioners into the have-a-lots and the have-littles.

121

Income support
In April 1988, the SB scheme will be divided in two. The system of weekly
SB payments will be renamed income support. (For the other part of the
new arrangements, see below). The new IS scheme will be calculated in the
same way as SB, and the basic weekly benefit rates continue. But, instead of
householder and non-householder rates, there will be a lower rate for single
childless people under 25 years old, regardless of whether they live with
their parents or maintain their own households. This seems to be a classic
case of administrative simplification triumphing over justice, fairness and
any sense of claimants' needs.

The main difference between SB and income support is that, instead of
attempting to meet individuals' varied needs through a medley of regulation-
based extra weekly payments, income support will cater for broad 'client
groups' on a rough and ready basis by giving them varying 'premia' on top
of the basic rates. Thus, the higher long-term SB rate is abolished, as are
the extra payments for heating, special diets, laundry and so on. Instead,
there are premia for families with a child or children, lone parents, pensioners, long-term sick and disabled people, and severely disabled people (the
last introduced in the final stages of the Bill's passage through Parliament,
to head off a more generous House of Lords amendment). There are, however, to be no premia for pregnancy or long-term unemployment, or for
people caring for the disabled or elderly.

The general effect is to 'average out' the needs of claimants in particular
groups, with the heaviest losses being suffered by those with the greatest
needs, and people who could previously claim the long-term SB rate. The
'simplification' is all on this side of the benefit equation. The administration of the means test will not be made simpler; indeed, some of the rules
will be more complex.

'Transitional protection' will be given: existing SB claimants in April
1988 who would qualify for a lower rate of income support will find that
their benefit, instead of being immediately reduced, will be frozen until
the new, lower rate for which they qualify catches up. In addition, the
'domestic assistance addition' (which can be claimed by some severely
disabled people) will be inflation-proofed. But, on the government's own
figures, losers will outnumber gainers.[8] Moreover, the official figures do
not take into account the loss of single payments – see below. This means
that losses, especially for families with children, will in reality be much
higher in many cases. And claimants will have to meet at least 20 per cent
of their rates, as well as water rates and some other costs, from their
benefit.

The social fund
One of the two sections of the social fund, covering payments for maternity
and funeral expenses, came into effect in April 1987 (see chapter 12). But
the major changes will be brought in in April 1988 – although, as Peter

122

Esam also points out, the way is being paved for the social fund by making cuts in the meantime.

Under the current SB scheme, claimants are entitled to lump-sum grants to meet specific needs, as laid down in regulations. Instead, the 'social fund' will replace these grants (single payments) and urgent needs payments with loans. It will be administered separately from weekly income support, and will also have different arrangements for challenging decisions, with no right to an independent appeal.

The main features of this part of the social fund are:

- most payments will be loans, not grants – the one exception being 'community care' payments, to help people to come out or stay out of institutional care;
- regulations will be replaced by 'guidance' from the secretary of state (ie, discretion);
- the fund will be cash limited;
- loans will be given for 'budgeting' difficulties and for 'financial crises' – in the case of the latter, claimants will be expected to look to other sources of help before getting a social fund loan;
- instead of each item needed being costed to obtain a total, a round sum will be given;
- there will no longer be an independent right of appeal against a decision on payment, but a system of review within the DHSS and subject to the same guidelines as the original decision.

The social fund was almost universally condemned when it was initially put forward, and opposition in Parliament was widespread – especially on the abolition of a right of appeal.[9] But ministers, determined to put a lid on the demand-led payments for SB claimants' needs, pressed ahead regardless. The social fund will succeed admirably in this aim. It is likely to be off-putting to claimants, who – even if they succeed in getting a payment – will find that in most cases all they get is a loan, which they have to pay back out of their benefit. The return to discretion will leave the door open to distinctions between the 'deserving' and 'undeserving' poor. And the abolition of a right of appeal marks a large step backwards in terms of claimants' rights.

But perhaps the most worrying aspect of the social fund is that the introduction of loans to replace most lump-sum grants represents not a bonus, as ministers would seem to be suggesting on occasions, but in effect a cut in weekly benefit. The Social Services Select Committee, in its report on the Green Paper, warned that the family premium, in particular, would need to be set at an adequate level in order for the social fund to be limited to exceptional cases, as the government was hoping.[10] The illustrative figures in the White Paper belied any hope that this might be achieved. The Social Security Advisory Committee (SSAC), in its recent report, returned to this crucial point: 'the social fund will be overwhelmed if the basic rates of weekly benefit are insufficient to meet regular and continuing needs'.[11]

But all the indications are that, given the likely benefit rates, and the imposition of the 20 per cent rates payment on all households, weekly benefit – already inadequate – *will* be insufficient. And, as SSAC also pointed out: 'there are many areas of capital expenditure which claimants cannot hope to meet from their weekly benefit' – in other words, the needs formerly met by single payments are not the exceptional expenses of a small minority, but the ordinary needs of many hard-pressed families on SB.[12]

Housing benefit

Both housing benefit (HB) and family credit will be aligned, more or less, with the new framework and rules for income support. All three benefits will be based on net income, not gross, and will include the same rules on the treatment of capital. The treatment of housing costs for those in and out of work will be the same for the first time. But this also means that any 'rough justice' in the new IS scheme will feed through into HB. However, unlike income support, there will be no 'transitional protection' for claimants on HB who will lose from the changes.

And there will be a lot of these. The main immediate 'savings' from the social security changes – £450 million in a full year – come from the cuts in HB, and will ensure in particular that hardly any working families at all will qualify any longer for HB. The imposition of sharper tapers (withdrawal rates) continues the trend of recent years described in chapter 12. The completely new element is the 20 per cent rates payment for all householders including HB claimants, with no compensating payment yet in sight. This has nothing to do with HB, and everything to do with the government's political aims relating to local authorities. But this is little comfort to those on HB, who are either out of work or on low pay and who are being used as pawns in the government's battles with local government.

Family credit and free school meals

The introduction of family credit to replace family income supplement (FIS) was heralded by the government as a major improvement for low paid families with children. Family credit will indeed be more generous, will go to twice as many people, and will cost about twice as much, as FIS – *if* the government optimistic estimate of a 60 per cent take-up rate is fulfilled.

But family credit will be taken into account for HB purposes; so some families will find that most or all of what they gain in family credit will be offset by a loss of HB. Some of the very poorest working families will, in fact, lose considerable weekly sums compared with their current position.[13] Moreover, the government is also proposing to abolish free school meals for everyone except those on income support. Families currently on FIS will receive compensation through the family credit rates; but this compensation is not generous, and will not prevent people living in areas where the price of school meals is high from losing out overall. And the very poorest families who are still receiving HB will find that much of the compensation for the loss of free school meals will be lost in lower HB entitlements.

The government's proud boasts about the generosity of family credit for low paid families with children sound rather hollow when set against its silence over the effects of these cuts on the incomes of precisely the same families. And one of the other main reasons why the government itself said that it was introducing family credit–to ensure that low paid workers recognised the amount of help they were getting from the state (and therefore modified their wage claims in return)–depended on the wage-earner receiving family credit in the wage packet. Once the government was forced to change its mind on the method of payment, and agreed to it being paid direct to the main carer instead, this advantage was irretrievably lost. It cannot happen very often that a central feature of government policy on wages is nullified by opposition from an 'unholy alliance' of employers' organisations, women's groups and the poverty lobby.

The Act in focus

Shackled from the start

The government's social security reviews were shackled from the start by the Treasury's stipulation that they were to be 'nil cost'–ie, that the changes must not result in higher expenditure on social security overall. Thus, any improvements in one area of benefits had to be paid for by cutbacks in another. Indeed, the reviews were to result, if possible, in 'savings' to finance future tax cuts. The reviews also perpetuated the artificial distinction between public spending on benefits and other goods and services, on the one hand, and tax expenditures, on the other. Thus, the review teams ignored the cost, and the distributional effects, of tax reliefs and tax allowances altogether.

These two limitations ensured that one of the government's main objectives–of 'targeting (available) resources on those in greatest need–would be hamstrung by the narrow definition of 'resources available'. Options were confined to those which proposed a redistribution of the existing social security budget, with no possibility of 'targeting' the wealth of the nation as a whole, either now or in the future, on the worst off.

Contradictory concepts

The major focus of the reforms, as the very structure of the Social Security Act makes clear, is a rationalisation of the present incoherent patchwork of means-tested benefits. Under the Social Security Act, means-tested benefits become the fulcrum of the social security system. There is a shift in the centre of gravity of the benefits system away from benefits as of right towards benefits requiring a 'test of income', as Norman Fowler likes to call it.

This is the major reason why the government cannot but fail in the aims

125

and objectives which it set itself. There is a limit to the extent to which means-tested benefits can be made 'simpler to understand and easier to administer'. They do not encourage 'self-reliance and independence'; on the contrary, being focussed on the poor, they must be withdrawn as incomes or savings rise, creating a ceiling which traps people into poverty, rather than a floor on which they can build by their own efforts.

Above all, means-tested benefits have failed in the past to achieve the central objective of 'targeting (available) resources on those who need them most'. Low take-up is an endemic problem of means-tested benefits (though not confined to them). In particular, the current FIS scheme only benefits one in two of those low paid families who could claim it.[14] As the Social Services Select Committee said in its response to the Green Paper: 'It is no use designing or "targeting" benefits if their target remains as elusive as ever.'[15] There is little evidence that the government has paid any attention to this fundamental problem.

Instead, the 'simplification' involved in the reforms will largely mean rougher justice – especially for those on income support, because of the bluntness of the proposed premia. 'Self-reliance' and 'independence' may mean less dependence on some state benefits, but is likely to mean more private dependence within the family, especially for women and young people, and more dependence on charities for those faced with the social fund. And 'targeting' means that gains by some groups of poor people will be accompanied by losses for others. On the government's own figures, nearly 4 million claimants of means-tested benefits will lose, compared with just over 2 million who will gain[16] – and these figures do not include the impact of the loss of single payments for those on income support. The interaction of some of the changes for working families means that the very poorest will lose out (with no 'transitional protection' to cushion the blow). The statistics, and the pattern of losses, make a mockery of the government's claim of 'targeting' resources, even leaving aside the narrow definition of 'resources' involved.

Ideology on the agenda
In addition to the Treasury's goal of making 'savings', various other objectives unrelated to the goals of a social security system became apparent during the progress of the reviews – even leaving aside the general political aim of creating a 'property-owning democracy', or 'people's capitalism', which pervaded the pensions debate.

The government's statement that the social security changes should be consistent with its economic objectives meant primarily that public spending should be reined it, to provide a system which 'the country can afford'. However, the government also wished the benefits system to fit in with its twin objectives of pricing the low paid into jobs, and of reining back pay increases. Thus, much was made of the 'unemployment trap', or 'better off out of work' problem, and of the generosity of the new family credit

126

scheme which would combat this. In addition, ministers sometimes argued for the conversion of single payments in the SB scheme into loans because low paid people in work had no such 'extras' available to them; and the original proposal that family credit should be paid through the pay packet was meant to aid the government's indirect incomes policy, by making visible to low paid workers the help they were getting from the state, so that they would reduce their wage demands.

The other political objective unrelated to social security provision was the government's desire to make high-spending local authorities more 'accountable' to their ratepayers. This–rather than ensuring an adequate income for those dependent on social security–was the rationale behind the proposal that all householders should pay at least 20 per cent of their rates. The poorest are the losers from this proposal, which represents a reversal of the 'targeting' principle which the government claimed was at the heart of its reforms.

A restricted remit

The Social Security Act embodies a very limited view of the role of social security, and was based upon reviews with a very restricted remit. First, as Francis Pym pointed out in the House of Commons, the 'first requirement' of a modern benefits system has not been fulfilled: the government made no attempt to assess the needs of those forced to depend on the social security system before readjusting the benefit rates of different groups of claimants.[17]

Secondly, no account has been taken in the reviews of the changes in society since the 1940s. In particular, the social security changes fail to recognise the reality of women's participation in the labour market, or their demand for financial independence. Similarly–although the proposed 'presence test' for income support was dropped after protests from many organisations–the benefits system in this country remains geared to the culture and behaviour patterns of the white majority and takes little account of the habits and life styles of people of other races.

Most fundamentally, however, the emphasis on means-tested benefits in the reforms betrays a dangerously narrow view of the functions of social security in the late twentieth century. The over-riding function of benefits is seen as the relief of poverty after it has occurred, rather than the prevention of poverty, the sharing of risks between the population as a whole or the transfer of resources between generations, between those with and without dependants, between the employed and the not-working or between the healthy and the sick.

Conclusion

The impact of the Social Security Act will be felt by many claimants and others in April 1988. The full force of some of the changes will be cushioned for a while by the 'transitional protection' afforded to income support claimants. But the longer-term effects of the government's 'reforms' are far-reaching and worrying to all those concerned about a fairer distribution of income in this country.

The downgrading of child benefit and the national insurance scheme, together with the expansion of private provision (especially in the pensions field) subsidised through tax benefits, and the greater emphasis on means-tested benefits, suggest a further development and consolidation of the divisions explored in various chapters of this book. On the one hand, the better-off will benefit from tax relief on their private pension schemes (and mortgages and other savings schemes, etc); on the other, the poor will be more reliant on 'poor relief' from means-tested benefits, the social fund and charities. We will be retreating ever further from Beveridge's aim of a benefits system 'for all citizens without distinction of rich and poor', providing 'security against want without a means test'. We will be advancing ever further towards a divided Britain.

CHAPTER 14

Conclusion I: A Divided Britain

Alan Walker

The conclusion to this pamphlet comprises two parts. In this chapter, we summarise the impact of Conservative policies on the poor and, in the final chapter, Ruth Lister sets out CPAG's responsible and wholly credible alternative to the present policies of impoverishment and inequality.

Where there is discord, may we bring harmony;
Where there is error, may we bring truth;
Where there is doubt, may we bring faith;
Where there is despair, may we bring hope.

(*St Francis of Assisi, quoted by Margaret Thatcher on election as prime minister, 4 May 1979*)

The government has 'done more than any other to bring the nation together'.

(*The prime minister, 8 January 1987*)

In 1983 the authors of *Thatcherism and the poor* were able only to draw tentative conclusions about the impact of the first four years of Conservative government on the poor. The main problem was lack of information on which to base firm conclusions. The government's general obscurantist attitude towards research was outlined in chapter one. Moreover, as the House of Commons Social Services Select Committee has reminded the DHSS annually for the past seven years,[1] very little information is collected by the Department with central responsibility for the bulk of the welfare state about the effects of policies on claimants and clients. The government's actions have further reduced the amount of information by which to assess and plan welfare services.

In addition, to be fair to the government, it might be argued that final assessments could not reasonably be made of the policies of an avowedly radical government after only one term of office. We must leave the academic historians to conduct a thorough examination of the phenomenon of 'Thatcherism' and to put it in proper historical context. For our part, it is legitimate to begin to draw firm conclusions about the impact of the Thatcher governments' policies on the poor, and despite the government's attempts to frustrate the search for truth, there is now ample evidence on which to base the judgements contained in this volume.

Divided Britain

The weight of authoritative evidence presented in the previous contributions builds up, chapter by chapter, to the overwhelming conclusion that Britain is a much more sharply divided society in 1987 than it was just eight years earlier. Let us be clear on two key points before proceeding to summarise the main dimensions of Mrs Thatcher's divided nation.

First, we are *not* arguing that social divisions based on class, race, gender and age began with the election of the Conservatives in 1979. What the authors of this volume are saying, however, is that the government *has* helped to widen and deepen these divisions, sometimes to a catastrophic extent.

Secondly, as we showed in chapters 1 and 2 and reiterate below, these increasing inequalities are not the accidental by-product of policies aimed at restoring Britain's fortunes, but are an essential component of the strategy being pursued by the government.

Britain is, officially, well into its sixth successive year of economic growth following the slump soon after the government came to power. Average living standards are at a record level and, to judge by the recent budget and the autumn statement on public expenditure which preceded it, there is plenty of revenue available for spending wherever the government considers it necessary. Yet, as the previous contributors have shown, there has been virtually no trickle-down effect on the incomes and living standards of the poor. In fact, the reverse is true: many of the poor have been getting poorer while the rich have been getting considerably richer. And, as *average* living standards have risen steadily and markedly, relative poverty has worsened.

The incredible theory, that if you pay 'telephone figure' salaries to boost growth then the poor will be better off than they would otherwise have been, has been exposed. However, for reasons of ideology and self-interest, some sections of the media and business community still promulgate the myth. Less credulous supporters of the government policy might have recognised that, rather than facilitating poor people's fair share of generally rising living standards, the clear intention has been to *detach* them from the average income escalator. Thus, one of the government's first actions on taking office was to abolish the link between earnings and pensions and other long-term benefits and, with it, the chance for poor families to benefit from the rising incomes of those in work.

The growth of poverty

The facts about poverty for those on benefit were reviewed in chapters 3 and 11. The burden of poverty has, in David Piachaud's words, 'increased grotesquely' over the last eight years.

130

- By 1984 nearly 8 million people were dependent on poverty level SB, compared with under 4 million in 1979.
- Between 1979 and 1985 the poorest families with children suffered a drop in the real value of their incomes of between 15.7 and 27.2 per cent (according to the number of children).
- The number of children taking free school meals rose from 898,768 (12 per cent of all pupils) in 1979 to 1,143,817 (18 per cent) in 1986, despite the cut back in entitlement under the 1980 Education Act.[2]

The meaning of life on SB is all too clear to those who experience it first hand: a struggle for existence (see chapter 11). A recent study of the spending patterns of poor families reiterated the findings of a long series of previous ones: children's diets were deficient in iron and calcium and it was impossible to maintain basic clothing standards.[3] The government has encouraged the better-off to accrue more and more wealth and possessions and has enlarged existing forms of consumption and created new ones, but at the same time it has persistently denied those reliant on benefits the chance to ease their plight.

Income and wealth
The gap between the top and bottom incomes of those in work has also widened dramatically and, again, the government has been actively supporting this trend. By allowing private sector firms to pay what they want and boosting higher incomes with generous tax cuts, while holding down public sector wages and reducing controls on low paying employers, the government has succeeded in reversing the post-war trend towards a slightly more equal distribution of income. Dominic Byrne meticulously details these changes in chapter 4.

- Between 1979 and 1986 the real level (adjusted for inflation) of earnings of men in the top tenth of the earnings league increased at more than five times the rate of those in the bottom tenth.
- Out of a total £12,000 million reduction in income tax since 1979, nearly half has gone to the top 10 per cent of taxpayers and only 3 per cent to the bottom 15 per cent. The average amount given away to those earning less than £5,000 per annum was £85, compared with £11,400 for those on £50,000 or more a year.

The historical trend for the top 1 per cent and 5 per cent of wealth holders to lose about 4 per cent of their share of total wealth each decade has been halted in the early 1980s.[4]

- The share of marketable wealth (homes, stocks, shares, etc) of the wealthiest 5 per cent, having dropped from 44 per cent in 1978 and 52 per cent in 1971, has held steady at 39 per cent since 1980.

Divided kingdom
The increasing divisions between rich and poor have been emphasised by

their geographical location. What is mistakenly referred to sometimes as the North/South divide is, as chapter 5 shows, not primarily spatial but social. Poor families are concentrated in certain parts of the country and the landscape of poverty reflects this.

- Official unemployment in the Northern region is double that in the South-east. In some local areas within these regions the unemployment rates differ by as much as eight times.
- The South-west has the highest percentage of full-time male employees earning less than £100 per week, yet the second highest percentage with incomes over £350 per week.

Contrary to Conservative propaganda about people pricing themselves out of jobs, the growth of unemployment in the deprived regions has gone hand in hand with a *fall* in average earnings.

- Between 1979 and 1986 male earnings in the North fell by 9 per cent, compared with those in the South-east.
- The proportion of men in the North, North-west and Yorkshire and Humberside being paid below the Council of Europe's decency theshold has more than doubled in the last seven years.

The government has abandoned regional policy in the face of the continued impoverishment of the North.

Unemployment
The growth of unemployment has been one of the major causes of the increase in poverty since 1979. Rather than simply being the by-product of a world recession, the British government has consciously chosen unemployment as a tool of social and economic policy.[5] It has been able to do so because the burden of unemployment is not borne equally. Thus, it is predominantly the same poor people in the benefit and low wage sectors who have experienced the lowest rises in income over the last eight years that have also been hit hardest by unemployment.

- Between 1979 and 1983 1.7 million jobs were lost in manufacturing industry, while banking, finance and insurance gained 122,000 new employees.
- 51 per cent of long-term unemployed men and 38 per cent of women are semi-skilled and unskilled, compared with only 4 per cent and 5 per cent, respectively, from higher professional and managerial groups.

The main response of the government to the increase in unemployment so necessary for its economic and social objectives has been, perversely, to cut unemployment benefit, increase special 'training' measures and a succession of attempts, 19 in all, artificially to reduce the headline unemployment count (see chapter 8). Together, these measures have removed one million people from the official monthly total – of course, these people are still unemployed but they are now statistically non-existent. Given the ease with which official unemployment can be 'reduced' in this way, it is, perhaps, not surprising that job creation has not been a priority. As David Taylor shows:

● On present performance it will take 30 years to provide a job for everyone wanting one and at least 15 years to bring unemployment down to the one million it was in 1979.

The widening health gap
The link between poverty and ill-health has been demonstrated conclusively by official and independent research (see chapter 9). A report prepared for the Health Education Council and, as yet unpublished, shows that children's health is deteriorating as poverty increases, the quality of school meals has declined and preventive medical services are cut back.[6] The British Medical Association has prepared a report which supports the key findings about the widening health gap between rich and poor in the HEC report and calls for a national commitment to tackle poverty and the sickness caused by deprivation: 'In the interests of both justice and public health there should be a national commitment to combat social inequalities and eliminate deprivation'.[7]

Unemployment is a crucial element in the growing health divide:

● The average *annual* mortality attributable to unemployment has been put at 2,125 men and 1,077 wives (see p75).

The link between unemployment and ill-health has been recognised by the government (see p 75). On the face of it, this is a remarkable admission – given that several thousand unnecessary deaths occur each year as a result of the government's policy of unemployment. However, it is not so much an admission of guilt as a testimony to the government's success in persuading the public, with the help of a credulous media, that it has no responsibility for unemployment.

Private affluence and public squalor
One of the main dimensions of the increased polarisation of British society, and a consistent theme in several chapters, is the growing gap between those reliant on the state and those who have access to private services. New forms of citizenship are being created. Underpinning the major polarisation between private affluence and public squalor is the government's antagonism towards the public sector.

The better-off, on average and above incomes and in secure employment, have experienced rising real incomes and are able to take part in the ever-expanding new forms of private consumption, such as out-of-town hypermarkets, information technology and multiple holidays. Consumption is facilitated by a rapidly increasing range of credit cards and opportunities to enhance savings at record interest rates. Alternatives are available to the

133

declining public services, including private medical insurance and residential and nursing homes.

The poor, on the other hand, are increasingly marginalised and stigmatised consumers (see chapter 11). They have to rely on low fixed incomes which are under attack (see chapters 12 and 13) and falling standards of public services (see chapter 10). The only opportunities for borrowing are from predatory loan sharks at exorbitant interest rates. Their consumption opportunities are being continually reduced and restricted as both low wages and the social wage are cut. The 'choice' for them is usually Hobson's choice: between food and shoes for the children, not, as it is for the better-off, *which* pair of shoes to add to an already plentiful stock.

On the one hand, the poor, dependent on state benefits, are told that their standards of living must be contained or even fall to maintain the incentive to work and to reduce the financial burden they are imposing on the state. So benefit provision is cut back (chapters 12 and 13) and growing numbers of claimants are stigmatised. On the other hand, the affluent are told they should have more in order to increase their incentives and to allow the economy to grow. To that end the state hand-outs made through the fiscal sector continue to grow.

Official attitudes, which sanction and legitimise this polarisation, make it quite clear which group contains the acceptable citizens and which does not. The affluent are congratulated by tax cuts, tax reliefs on fringe benefits and public asset share hand-outs; while the poor are too often branded as feckless and fraudulent (chapter 11).

The government's privatisation policy has been a major motivating force behind the formation of these new classes of citizenship and the polarisation between them. For example, the standards of the public social services have declined and the poor are expected to fund an increasing proportion of services themselves as charges are increased. The best known example of this creeping privatisation is the twelve-fold increase in prescription charges since 1979 (only partially mitigated by free prescriptions), but there are plenty of other instances: school meals, council house rents, bus fares and home help charges. The direct sale of public sector utilities has also reinforced this trend, as share give aways increase the wealth of the better-off and, once privatised, the poor pay for the change in terms of wage cuts (see chapter 4) and increased charges. There is also evidence that, once public utilities are privatised, they harden their attitude towards the poor. For example, in 1986, disconnections by British Gas increased by 27 per cent to 45,255, compared with an increase of only 1 per cent in electricity disconnections.[8]

Poor and marginalised
Two groups of poor people – women and blacks – have been singled out for particularly harsh treatment by the Conservative government. As Caroline Glendinning shows, unemployment among women has increased more

sharply than among men. Moreover, women bear the main burden of the impact of unemployment and poverty within the family. In work their minimal employment rights have been reduced significantly by dint of government policy (chapter 6).

The attitude towards women of the government headed by Britain's first woman prime minister is crystal clear. They provide a ready-made pool of part-time labour – a reserve army – and their rights to work can be cut in the interests of enhancing the profitability of private (often privatised) enterprise. In Edwina Currie's words, women are 'cheap and plentiful'.[9]

Black people, especially black women, have been further marginalised and stigmatised.

- The unemployment rate for black men and women is twice that for their white counterparts.
- The average weekly earnings of male workers, in 1982, were £129 for white men, compared with £109.20 for Afro-Caribbeans and £88 for Bangladeshi men.

There is, as Hilary Arnott reports, ample evidence of discrimination in the labour market against those from ethnic minorities.

The politics of inequality

This catalogue of inequalities and increased social divisions, detailed in previous chapters and summarised here, results in part directly from government policies. There is, in other words, a systematic policy to pursue and exploit inequality. The government views inequality as being helpful to incentives at both ends of the income distribution and does not regard gross disparities in income and wealth as a problem. On the contrary, it sees it as a measure of success. In Lord Young's words:

> If some occupations are less highly valued then this gives encouragement to people to work in occupations where they are more highly valued. This is a fair system not in the sense that earnings are equal but the individuals enjoy equal opportunities to earn.[10]

The policy of two nations has been pursued remorselessly since 1979. The government has exacerbated changes in the distribution of industry and employment and the increasing segmentation of the labour market, rather than attempted to ameliorate them as previous governments have done. As we have seen, the division between the majority in relatively secure employment and the minority of unemployed has been a primary focus for the government's two nation politics.

Rather than seeking to unite the nation, the Conservative government has increased the polarisation between what A.H. Halsey has called the 'prosperous majority in secure and increasingly well-remunerated employment' and the 'depressed minority of the unemployed, the sick, the old, and the unsuccessful ethnic minorities'.[11] This polarisation has been characterised as the 'one-third/two-thirds society'.[12] The open rationalisation for this politics of inequality is that the poor will benefit from an overall increase in living standards. Again, according to Lord Young:

> Successful enterprise does bring material reward in society. General standards of living rose steadily and substantially through most of the Victorian era ... So in looking at the generation of Victorian entrepreneurs and at the results of their achievements, *we need not feel guilty that their success was at the expense of the poor.*

This brazen denial of guilt about poverty is characteristic of the government and, as we showed earlier, it is completely impervious to the overwhelming evidence that its confidence in the free play of market forces is misplaced. In crude political terms the detached and marginalised poor are, quite simply, irrelevant to the sort of society the government is trying to create and its own political future.

What future for the poor?

What would be the impact on the poor of a third term of Thatcher government? The Conservative Manifesto for the next election was not available at the time of writing but there are some clear indications about future directions.

Selective social security: As Fran Bennett points out, proposals and legislation in the pipeline will increase the means-testing of benefits and, therefore, the stigma attached to claiming. Remarkably, in the post-war period the government has openly planned to reduce the incomes of 3.8 million poor people (including 200,000 couples with children and 250,000 lone parents) in order to redistribute the resources to those judged to be in 'greatest need'.

The cut in housing benefit, from 6 April 1987, and the abolition of single payments for baby things and the maternity grant provide an indication of what is in store. The latest cut in housing benefit deprived 350,000 households of more than £1 a week and 980,000 of between 50 pence and £1, while 110,000 households lost housing benefit altogether.[14] Over the past four years, 1.36 million households have been excluded from housing benefit. This is another example of horizontal redistribution between relatively poor people rather than vertical redistribution from rich to poor. Under another Thatcher government there appears to be little chance of increasing the incomes of the poor relative to the rich and any real increases for some groups will be funded by cuts in the incomes of other poor people.

Dismantling elements of the welfare state: The increase in public expenditure

136

announced in the 1986 autumn statement is likely to prove a temporary pre-election switch in a policy of restriction over seven successive years. Public housing has been particularly savaged: subsidies to council tenants were cut by 31 per cent between 1979 and 1985, compared with an increase in the subsidy to owner-occupiers of 212 per cent. In 1978, 107,000 council houses were built in Britain, whereas in 1986 the total was 31,000. The number of homeless people has increased from 41,000 in 1979 to 140,000 in 1984 - more than in the Victorian late nineteenth century. The proposed community charge will be particularly onerous for poor families. In this and other areas of the welfare state - such as the legal aid system[15] - the poor can expect to be required to fund an increasing proportion of declining public services.

Dear prudence: Perhaps the clearest indication of what the poor could expect from a third bout of Thatcherism is the government's budget strategy. The much acclaimed prudence of the Chancellor[16] will cost the poor dear. By definition tax cuts are biased against the very lowest paid - in 1984 there were 250,000 low paid workers with children and 300,000 childless workers with incomes *below* the tax threshold - and the government has emphasised this bias by cutting the top rates of tax and raising the bottom.[17] As Michael Prowse observed following the 1986 budget: 'Further cuts in the basic rate of tax, as favoured by the Chancellor, would continue this redistribution from rich to poor'.[18]

At the heart of this strategy is not only the belief in inequality discussed above but also an aversion to public services. It is *not* that there are no resources available for increasing the incomes of the poor and improving public services - the government has spent £12,000 million on tax cuts since 1979, mortgage interest relief has risen to £4,500 million and defence expenditure has more than doubled - but the government has successfully created the impression that these improvements cannot be afforded. In doing so, it has also manufactured a perverse notion of prudence which is over-generous to the rich and parsimonious towards the poor.

Living with unemployment: All the evidence suggests that the government is content to go on living with unemployment, providing that the politically sensitive headline monthly count can be contrived to fall. This spells disaster for unemployed people and their families: all they have to look forward to is biting poverty, ill-health and premature death.

Regardless of what the government says publicly about the priority it gives to reducing unemployment, in private it is *planning* for unemployment to remain at present levels up to 1990.[19] A recent National Economic Development Council report emphasised this by pointing out that the government's main measures cannot solve the problem of unemployment.[20] This suggests, too, that the government intends to remain impervious to the effects of the fractures it has opened up between the regions and nations of the British Isles.

Instead of job creation, as both David Taylor and Ruth Lister argue, the unemployed can expect a continued stress on 'workfare' schemes and attempts to cajole them into low wage jobs.[21] While Lord Gowrie, a former employment minister, does not regard £33,000 per annum as a living wage, a refusal to accept weekly wages of £50 – below the legal minimum set by wages councils – is regarded as sufficient for disqualification from benefit.

Rebuilding one nation

Eight years of Conservative government have fostered widespread passivity and resignation and, moreover, have succeeded in reducing significantly public expectations about what governments can achieve. Thus, there is much for those campaigning against poverty to overcome. The essential elements for success are a viable alternative policy and a realisation that the extent to which the Thatcher government has changed the character and beliefs of the British people has been considerably overstated.

In the following chapter Ruth Lister outlines CPAG's alternative to the government's two nations policies and shows that there is strong support among the British public for collective services. There is support, too, for reducing the inequalities between rich and poor that the government has done so much to widen. In the London Weekend TV national survey, 74 per cent of those interviewed said that the gap between rich and poor was too wide.[22]

It is important to build on this egalitarian impulse and, at the very least, re-establish a consensus about the redistribution of income and wealth and, most importantly, about the basic function of social and economic policy to promote the welfare of the whole nation. The government claims that it has restored the foundations of British prosperity. But no building constructed on such divisions will survive very long and no economy can be regarded as prosperous until poverty and unemployment have been genuinely eradicated and everyone is able to share in the fruits of economic growth. If policy-makers are seriously interested in re-building one nation, the social and economic priorities of the last eight years must be reversed and a priority given to the interests of the poor.

CHAPTER 15

Conclusion II: There is an alternative

Ruth Lister

The prospects for Divided Britain

'Britain as a nation is becoming increasingly divided, anxious and embittered.'[1]

This is the observation of a former Conservative minister. It sums up the growing concern about the direction in which Britain is heading and inevitably raises questions about the implications for our society of a third Conservative term.

Earlier chapters have outlined the impact of Conservative policies since 1979 and have suggested likely policy developments if the Conservatives are re-elected. These are clearest in the social security field where the Social Security Act 1986, due to be implemented in April 1988, is already on the statute book. As Fran Bennett's chapter makes clear, the Act represents a further shift in the centre of gravity of social security policy so that means-tested benefits are now explicitly presented as the fulcrum of the social security system.

In addition, Lord Young, the employment secretary, has confirmed that, if re-elected, the government is considering withdrawing the right to social security benefits from unemployed 16- and 17-year-olds on the basis that they should all accept places on the Youth Training Scheme. Fears have also been raised that the government might introduce some form of the notorious American 'Workfare' scheme, under which the unemployed have to work for their benefits, possibly by making the Job Training Scheme compulsory (see chapter 8, which discusses how far down this road the government has already travelled). At present, this has been denied on the grounds that there would not be sufficient work available, but support for the idea has come from a junior employment minister.[2]

According to the *Daily Express*, a reliable barometer of Conservative opinion, cuts in benefits for the unemployed constitute a key part of phase three of 'the Thatcher revolution' which will mark 'a radically new approach to social issues':[3] Other elements of this 'new approach' include, according to the *Express*, the replacement of domestic rates by a regressive flat rate poll tax (or 'community charge' as the government euphemistically calls it); the decontrol of private rents; the selling off of inner-city housing estates; and the sale of state-owned assets such as water and electricity.

139

At the same time, the Chancellor has made clear his determination further to reduce the basic and higher rates of income tax – probably drastically in the case of the latter. Reports have suggested that there might, at the same time, be a further shift in the tax burden on to VAT, as in 1979.[4] Less clear now is the government's attitude towards the reform of personal taxation to remove sex discrimination from the tax system, discussed in chapter 6. In the wake of a decidedly lukewarm response to its proposal for a system of transferable tax allowances (under which a married person could transfer any unused tax allowance to their spouse), the financial secretary to the Treasury announced during the budget debate that the government would consider the matter further to see if there were 'any satisfactory halfway house' to the approach in the original Green Paper. This might point to a system of partially transferable allowances under which only part of an unused allowance could be transferred.[5]

So, the general prospect is of a growing divide between those able to enjoy the property and share-owning democracy which is the prime minister's goal and the growing ranks of the poor who are excluded from it. A gulf is opening up between skilled workers at the 'core' of the labour market and the unskilled; the 'peripheral' part-time and temporary workers; and the unwaged as changes in the labour market are accentuated and accelerated by government economic and social policy.[6] Whilst comfortable Britain is protected by improved private provision and the tax reliefs that subsidise it, public provision is likely to be increasingly confined to the poor. As Malcolm Wicks, director of the Family Policy Studies Centre has warned, we are moving towards:

> a residual welfare state, characterised by increasing inequality, deepening poverty and greater reliance on the means test, a growing role for the private market and, consequently, social division and conflict.[7]

And all the time, the rich look set to grow even richer.

'The spirit of collective obligation'

The apparent success of 'Thatcherism' in capturing 'hearts and minds' in the late 1970s has been attributed, in part, to the clear vision it presented of the kind of society it wished to create. Any alternative strategy must similarly be grounded in a clear vision of social change and social relations; and proposals for the reform of the welfare state must be based on a clear set of principles.

At the heart of the debate on the future of the welfare state lies the tension between the responsibility of the individual and of the community as a whole for the welfare of each and every member of society. The Church of England's *Faith in the city* report pointed to the dangers of the growing emphasis on individual responsibility:

140

The main assumption on which present economic policies are based is that prosperity can be restored if individuals are set free to pursue their own economic salvation. The appeal is to economic self-interest and in-dividualism . . . Individual responsibility and self-reliance are excellent objectives. The nation cannot do without them. But pursuit of them must not damage a collective obligation and provision for those who have no choice, or whose choices are at best forced ones. We believe that at present too much emphasis is being given to individualism, and not enough to collective obligation. In the absence of a spirit of collective obligation or the political will to foster it, there is no guarantee that the pursuit of innumerable individual self-interests will add up to an im-provement in the common good.[8]

The 'spirit of collective obligation' – based on an understanding of our mutual inter-dependence – needs to be rekindled. We need to go back to basics and remind people of the purpose of the welfare state in general and the social security system in particular. It is not simply there to provide a safety net for the poor. As the Social Policy Committee of the Church of England's Board of Social Responsibility argued, a serious risk of such a model of the welfare state is that it,

> could lead to a system of public welfare which would become a form of public charity to keep people from sinking below the breadline rather than a means for tackling the persistent reality of poverty and for ensur-ing that all can participate fully as citizens in society. The danger of the state involving itself only in the care of those who cannot care for themselves is that those people begin to be seen as failures and that welfare provision then becomes a one-way relationship of giving by the better off and receiving by the poor.[9]

At the same time, the large sums received by the better-off in the form of tax relief remain obscured.

The broader functions of the welfare state lie in:

- the guarantee of genuine security against risks such as unemployment, ill-health or disability and contingencies such as old age;
- the sharing of responsibility for raising the next generation and for car-ing for dependants so that it does not fall solely on the shoulders of in-dividual women and families.

Within that broader framework, the social security system, in conjunc-tion with the tax system, represents an important tool for the redistribution of resources along a number of dimensions:

- from better-off to worse-off;
- from those without children to those with children;
- from waged to unwaged;
- from healthy to sick;

141

- within the family, from men to women;
- over the lifecycle of each individual, so that people have more money during periods such as child-rearing and old age when without such redistribution income tends to be low relative to needs.

Taking these functions together, they add up to a welfare state which aims to prevent poverty and not simply relieve it after the event. In practical terms, this means benefits and services which are available to everyone on equal terms, rather than benefits and services which are confined to the poor. As Richard Titmuss observed more than two decades ago, benefits and services which are for the poor alone soon become poor benefits and services. They isolate the poor so that the rest of society no longer has a real stake in defending and improving the residualised and stigmatised welfare state.

Social security and social citizenship

Central to the principles which CPAG believes should govern any reform of the social security system is the concept of 'social citizenship'. The term originated with T.H. Marshall, who wrote of progress 'from the right to a modicum of economic welfare and security to the right to share to the full in the social heritage and to live the life of a civilised being according to the standards prevailing in the society'.[10] For the social security scheme to ensure full social citizenship for all members of society a number of conditions must be satisfied:

- Benefits must be high enough to ensure that no one is excluded from full participation in the life of society by lack of money. This means the assessment of need must take account of social and cultural as well as basic physical needs, in the development of what Professor Peter Townsend has termed a 'participation standard'.

- Full social citizenship requires the recognition of the right to autonomy of individual adults, in particular women. This means treating the individual rather than the couple as the basic unit for both social security and tax purposes.

- Everyone should have equal access to, and equal treatment from, the social security system regardless of race, sex, marital status or sexual orientation. Benefit levels should not, as at present, discriminate against any one category of claimants such as the unemployed. The creation of a non-racist social security system depends not just on the elimination of overt discrimination and prejudice but also on the development of the flexibility to take account of cultural differences.

- The dignity of all those who claim benefits must be respected. This means that people must have clear rights to benefits. The system must be administered efficiently and courteously. This is not possible unless there

142

are enough well trained and well paid staff to do the job properly in a decent environment – at least equivalent, say, to those found in a bank or building society. It is high time that what the DHSS's own *Handbook of Good Practice* calls the 'two nations' of supplementary benefit and contributory benefit caller sections is ended.

● Benefits should be as easy to understand and to administer as possible.

● Thought needs to be given to ways in which claimants can have a greater say in how the social security system is run. 'User control' in the welfare state is a popular slogan in some quarters these days, but little attempt has been made to think through its implications for the social security system.

A four-pronged anti-poverty strategy

Before turning to look more specifically at the reform of social security, it is important to set such reform in context. The weight of tackling poverty and inequality cannot fall exclusively on the social security system. There are at least three other prongs to an effective anti-poverty strategy:

1. *Taxation*

● At present, all but the top 4 or 5 per cent of taxpayers face the same basic rate of tax. A more progressive tax structure, with more rates than at present, is needed. A first step would be the reintroduction of a reduced rate tax band on the first slice of taxable income.

● Independent taxation of husband and wife is a priority. Each partner should be eligible for the same personal allowance. The money saved from abolishing the married man's tax allowance should be used to improve child benefit and a number of other social security benefits.[11]

● All tax reliefs and allowances should be set against the basic rate only so as not to give the highest paid an extra advantage. In the longer term, non-personal tax reliefs should be phased out altogether as part of a comprehensive income tax under which all income is taxable (see also pages 148-50).

● National insurance contributions should be aligned with income tax so that they become, in effect, a social security tax. In particular, the regressive ceiling on the income on which contributions are payable should be abolished.

● More effective taxation of capital transfers and a wealth tax are needed to ensure a fairer distribution of wealth.

2. *Employment*

While social security and tax reform are vital, the key determinants of most people's incomes are wages and salaries and people's access to them. There are severe limits on the extent to which the tax and social security systems can compensate for gross inequalities in the distribution of original income. These must therefore also be tackled at source:

- Low pay should be dealt with by means of a statutory minimum wage and improved equal pay laws.

- The creation of jobs and expansion of employment opportunities must be the top priority for economic policy.

- Access to employment must be improved for groups who are disadvantaged in the labour market. This includes, for example, ethnic minorities, people with disabilities and women.

3. *Public services*

A fairer distribution of incomes needs to be backed up by, and in some cases is dependent on, an infra-structure of good quality public services. For example:

- An expansion of and improvement in child care facilities is crucial to improving women's access to jobs.

- The key to tackling fuel poverty lies in a national insulation scheme which could build on the important work done so far by the voluntary schemes.

- The poverty experienced by many is exacerbated by inadequate housing or even, in a growing number of cases, homelessness. There needs to be a commitment to making a reality of the right to decent housing for all to which successive post-war governments have paid lip-service.

- The links between poverty and unemployment and ill-health have been stressed elsewhere in this pamphlet. Tackling poverty and unemployment directly must be a major element in breaking that link. But there must also be an adequately resourced health service committed to the development of preventative policies designed to reduce inequalities in health.

Reforming social security

While recognising the importance of the other elements of a coherent and comprehensive anti-poverty strategy, it is social security that is central to CPAG's work and on which we therefore focus now.

Our long-term goal for social security is a comprehensive system of non-means-tested, non-contributory benefits which genuinely meet the needs of those unable to derive an income from paid employment. Each individual would receive benefit in his or her own right. Children's needs would be covered by a more generous child benefit scheme that provided the same benefit regardless of whether their parent(s) are in or out of paid employment.

We recognise that the gap between our goal and the reality of the present system is very wide. It would be unrealistic to think that it could be bridged overnight. But, unlike some other proposals for reform, it does not require a 'big bang' solution that starts again from scratch. Instead, it could be introduced in stages, building on the best elements of the present system.

144

However, a clear programme with stated targets would be essential to avoid the kind of adhocery that has all too often passed for social security reform in the past.

We do not attempt to spell out such a programme here. We merely outline what we believe should be its main elements:

● A phased increase in child benefit to a level which is high enough to make a special addition for children in other social security benefits unnecessary. Much of the cost of this could be met from the resources freed by the abolition of the married man's tax allowance. Once child benefit is paid at an adequate level (and we have achieved a more progressive tax system), the case for making it taxable becomes more compelling, although there are still arguments against this which have to be noted.

● The removal of the discrimination against the unemployed in the national insurance scheme, so that unemployment benefit rather than supplementary benefit becomes their main source of support. This means raising unemployment benefit to the same level as invalidity benefit after six months and paying it for as long as unemployment lasts.

● The development of a disability income scheme which includes a disability costs element as well as providing an income for those unable to take full-time paid work.

● Adequate provision during maternity and for those caring for dependants, with special help for one-parent families in the interim.

● A phased increase in national insurance benefits to a level which enables full participation in society. Work still needs to be done to establish precisely what such levels would need to be, though existing research provides some pointers.[12] Once those benefits, which replace wages, are adequate and the tax system is fairer, they should be made taxable.

● Contribution tests should be phased out.

● Housing benefit should be reformed so that tenants and owner-occupiers are treated the same. This would involve pooling the resources currently spent on mortgage interest tax relief with the housing benefit budget.

● An allowance should be introduced for all young people in education or training after school-leaving age.

Our immediate priorities are an improvement in child benefit and extra help for the long-term unemployed. At the same time, while the aim in the longer term is to remove the need for means-tested supplementary benefit, except as a genuine emergency safety net, shorter term improvements will have to be made to the scheme. In particular, there is an urgent need for the children's scale rates to be raised, the higher long-term rate to be extended to the unemployed, and the quality of service to be improved.

As our broadsheet 'There *is* an alternative' recognises, the above goals raise a number of important questions. These are explored in greater depth in the forthcoming report of CPAG's Anti-Poverty Working Party. More detailed suggestions for short-term alternatives to the Social Security Act 1986 are contained in a Social Security Consortium paper.[13]

The Opposition parties' alternatives

This report has, inevitably, focused on the present government's record. When discussing the alternatives to it, it is appropriate to look also at what the main opposition parties are proposing to do about poverty as spelt out in published documents.[14] It is heartening that both the Labour Party and the Liberal/SDP Alliance appear to agree with us that the attack on poverty must be a priority for any incoming government. However, we are unable to give an unqualified welcome to either party's proposals for reform.

The Liberal/SDP Alliance

The Alliance is proposing an immediate 'three-pronged attack on poverty'. The first two prongs are an improvement in child benefit and pensions. The third is a plan 'to build on and ultimately replace FIS, SB and free school meals and milk with a single and larger basic benefit'.[15] In the longer term, the means-testing of the basic benefit will be applied through the tax system. A carer's benefit and further improvements to child benefit are also promised. The exact balance which the Alliance would aim for as between the means-tested basic benefit and child benefit and national insurance benefits is not yet clear – the SDP has called the means-tested basic benefit the 'centrepiece' of its proposed reforms, whereas the Liberal Party appears to be less enthusiastic about this approach, as Archy Kirkwood made clear in his interview for *Poverty* (Summer 1986).

The Alliance's approach is very different from that outlined earlier in this chapter in two main respects. First and foremost, we have always made clear that we cannot support the shift towards greater selectivity, which is central to the SDP's approach to social security reform and which has now been adopted by the Alliance, albeit in a weakened form. This approach is inconsistent with the principles for reform that we have put forward. We are sceptical of the claims that a computerised, integrated selective system, such as the Alliance advocates, can solve the problems inherent in means-testing. While it should reduce the problem of take-up, we do not believe that it will completely solve it. The extension and, to some degree, rationalisation of means-testing will, in fact, draw more people into the poverty trap and will sharpen its practical impact. We are also concerned that the proposed basic benefit scheme will be insufficiently flexible to cope with the fluctuating circumstances typical of many low income families.

Second, the Alliance makes clear its belief that poverty and low pay 'should be dealt with through the tax and benefit system'. Its only concession towards direct action to tackle low pay at its roots is a recognition of 'a role for reformed wages councils, whose agreements are properly enforced, to protect and enhance the pay and conditions of service of the most vulnerable employees such as part-time and home-based workers and younger employees'.[16] A minimum wage is rejected, even though the Liberal Party had earlier advocated it as a complement to its tax credit proposals. As it is, the proposed basic benefit scheme could serve to underpin and encourage low wages, for employers will know that the state is willing to subsidise them through a more efficient and extensive mechanism than the current family income supplement.

Despite our differences of approach, a number of the Alliance's specific proposals are welcome. In particular, child benefit appears still to have a relatively high priority and we are pleased that our criticisms of the original plan to make it taxable have been taken into account. Less welcome is the fact that an initial increase of only £1 is now promised. It is also worth noting that the Alliance is prepared to abandon contribution tests and replace them with a 'single and more generous work test', of which details are not yet available.

Although the Alliance combines its tax and benefit reforms, including the merging of tax and national insurance contributions, the actual proposals for creating a fairer income tax structure are fairly limited. There is a commitment to independent taxation and the phasing out of the married man's tax allowance, although it appears that this is no longer an immediate priority. Otherwise, the only change proposed is the restriction of mortgage interest tax relief to the basic rate of tax–not quite the vigorous attack on the hidden welfare state of tax reliefs and allowances that CPAG would like to see.

The Labour Party

One important lesson that the Labour Party has learnt is that an attack on poverty cannot be launched from the DHSS alone, although the full extent of the need for cross-departmental coordination is, perhaps, not yet fully appreciated. Proposals for the reform of social security and of taxation have been developed together, and have been linked with the party's plans for low pay, in particular the commitment to introduce a statutory minimum wage.

On the taxation front, the elements of a more progressive tax and national insurance structure are outlined. An important part of the package is the introduction of independent taxation for women and men. Although the proposal for the redistribution of resources from the married man's tax allowance into child benefit does not go as far as CPAG has advocated, it does represent a reasonable compromise between those in the Labour Party supporting CPAG's position and those who opposed any switch of resources from the married man's allowance into child benefit.

On social security, CPAG has already welcomed the Labour Party's emergency package, which includes improvements in child benefit, pensions and the position of the long term unemployed, and the first stage of a phased disability income scheme. This would be financed by raising revenue from the top 5 per cent of taxpayers who, as we saw in chapter 4, have gained disproportionately from tax cuts since 1979. Similarly, the longer term aims 'to end completely the present means-tested system of benefits' and to provide 'benefits for women in their own right' are in line with CPAG's own goals.

However, what is lacking is any sense of what the path from short-term reform to longer-term aims would look like and exactly how the aims would be achieved. Thus, many important areas of policy are not addressed except by a passing reference. No clear targets are set for future benefit levels. There is also considerable disappointment that no notice appears to have been taken of the growing demand within the Labour Party that it should abandon its commitment to the contributory principle. Instead, there is simply a vague promise to 'look at ways of reducing the numbers of those who do not fully benefit from national insurance – such as women, part-time workers, the self-employed and the very low paid'.[17]

Perhaps most worrying is the implication in the NEC statement on social security and taxation presented to the 1986 conference that further progress, over and above the emergency package, will be dependent on economic growth. It states that 'as our national wealth grows, we intend to make progress, as fast as resources allow, towards more far-reaching objectives'. Welcome as the initial £3.6 billion package is, it hardly exhausts the potential for redistribution of a government committed to a fairer allocation of income and wealth.

A commitment to redistribution

The limited nature of the Opposition parties' commitment to redistribution reflects a long-standing tendency on both Left and Right to subordinate social policy to economic policy.[18] In our view this is short-sighted and misguided. Of course, economic policy is important, but it is not an end in itself. It is a means to building a better society and social policy is critical to that task. As the Church of England Board for Social Responsibility observed:

> Of course the creation of wealth is important . . . But the question remains: for what is that wealth to be used? . . . The well-being of all members of that society cannot just be an incidental consequence of an economic policy but must be an integral part of the overall policy which decides in which direction our society should be heading. Only in this way can a proper relationship be reached between economic and social policy.[19]

Indeed, it is arguable that policies devoted to the creation of greater social cohesion and solidarity would provide a firmer basis for economic growth

148

than our currently divided society. As David Donnison has argued, 'a good welfare state, far from being a burden on the productive economy, provides the essential political basis for sound economic policies'.[20]

We have already conceded that the kind of reforms we are advocating cannot be achieved overnight. It is also true that economic growth would be helpful in meeting some of the costs; and that the lower the level of unemployment, the easier it will be to fund a decent social security scheme. Past experience shows, however, that while growth might lead to a general improvement in living standards, the 'trickle down' effect to the poor is limited and the gap between their living standards and those of the majority tends to widen. And this is exactly what has happened between 1981 and 1987. The poor cannot, therefore, depend on or wait for significant economic growth. A start must be made *now*. Whether or not strong economic growth is achieved, there must be a clear commitment to redistribution.

The scope for redistribution is greater than is often realised. As Dominic Byrne's chapter made clear, the present government has shown the way, albeit in the wrong direction. Apart from reversing the substantial redistribution to the rich that has taken place in recent years, there are a number of possible sources of revenue for funding a phased anti-poverty programme. These include.

● *The hidden welfare state of tax reliefs and allowances.* Very large sums of money are bound up in this hidden welfare state which, by and large, benefits the better-off in our society. For example, mortgage interest tax relief and the married man's tax allowance each cost well over £4 billion. The cost to the taxpayer of tax relief on private pensions is greater than that of the basic retirement pension. These are resources that could, in a phased programme of redistribution, be put to better use. At a minimum, if all tax reliefs and allowances were set against the standard rate of tax only, it would save £1.4 billion (at 1986/7 tax rates).[21]

● *The ceiling on national insurance contributions.* As already noted, this ceiling means that the highest paid pay a lower proportion of their earnings in contributions than the low paid. If the ceiling were abolished, it would raise nearly £1 billion.[22]

● *Wealth and capital taxes.* The distribution of wealth is very unequal. The recent increase in the yield from capital taxes should not be allowed to mask the fact that they have been weakened under the present government. It is officially estimated that the yield from capital taxes in 1986/7 would have been £835 million higher if the 1978/9 tax regime had still held.[23] Although the amount of revenue that could be raised from a wealth tax and the strengthening of capital taxes is not huge, neither is it insignificant.

● *Fringe benefits and tax evasion.* Tax revenues would be higher if greater priority were given to a crackdown on tax evasion. On the Institute for Fiscal Studies' estimates, the Inland Revenue could be losing up to £5 billion a year in unpaid taxes. Other estimates are even higher.[24] And there is no reason why fringe benefits should not be taxed similarly to earned income.

They have continued to flourish in recent years despite the cuts in higher tax rates in 1979 which were supposed to make them less 'necessary'.

Building public support

The identification of possible sources of revenue is an important step in building public support for a concerted attack on poverty. For too long the message has been that the 'country cannot afford it'. Until fairly recently, there has been a lot of exaggerated talk of a public expenditure crisis in the welfare state. At a time when the Chancellor is able to 'give away' over £2 billion in cutting the basic rate of tax, it is clear that we *can* afford to start tackling poverty. The question is whether we choose to do so.

The present government has made it clear that its priority is further cuts in taxation. Opinion polls suggest that this priority is not shared by the majority of the population. For example, after the 1986 budget, a Gallup Poll commissioned by *New Society* asked whether the 1p cut in the basic rate of tax or increasing benefits to the poor should have had higher priority. The results showed that 61 per cent favoured increasing benefits; only 27 per cent favoured the tax cut.

More generally, the British Social Attitudes Survey found that the proportion in favour of increasing taxes and spending more on housing, education and social benefits rose from 32 per cent in 1983 to 45 per cent in 1985; while the proportion in favour of cutting taxes and spending less on welfare went down from 9 per cent to 6 per cent. It also found that about seven out of ten people believed government 'had a responsibility to reduce income differences between rich and poor'; only a quarter disagreed.

As one of the contributors to the 1986 British Social Attitudes Report commented, ' "Collectivism" seems to be an integral feature of public attitudes in this country, shared by those of quite differing ideological viewpoints on other issues'.[25] It is easy to lose sight of this 'collectivist' seam in public opinion when politicians continually appeal to individual self-interest. The challenge facing us in this Election is to tap that seam and the growing public concern about the widening gap between the 'haves' and the 'have-nots' in divided Britain.

Four years ago, in *Thatcherism and the poor*, we made an appeal to all those in positions of influence to help us to ensure that the interests of the poor were not neglected in the run up to the 1983 Election. Their interests were neglected then and have been in the years which followed. As the evidence of the growing divide between rich and poor and the severe consequences for the health and well-being of the latter mounts, and the opinion polls register growing public disquiet about the poverty and inequality which are disfiguring our society, it would be a tragedy if the interests of those living in poverty were neglected yet again. It is over the coming weeks and months that the agenda for the next government will be set. It is the responsibility of each and every one of us to ensure that the fight against poverty and inequality and for a fairer society is at the top of that agenda.

Mrs Thatcher's diary
Policies affecting poor families:
May 1979–April 1987

Huw Edwards*

(see p iv for abbreviations used)

1979

June: Budget: income tax cuts benefited the highest paid most; tax cuts outweighed by increase in VAT for those on average earnings or below; prescription charges raised from 20p to 45p and some dental charges raised; 50p increase in one-parent benefit but no increase in CB.

September: Social Security (Claims and Payments) Amendment Regulations: UB henceforth to be paid fortnightly, except for those on short-time working or who choose to be paid weekly.

November: Previous year's shortfall in uprating of short-term benefits not made good. Pensions and other long-term benefits not fully protected against increase in VAT.

1980

February: Price of a school meal raised from 30p to 35p. 1,050 extra DHSS staff employed on anti-fraud work.

March: Budget: CB to be increased by 75p in November but £1.20 increase required to restore April 1979 value; instead, improvements made in one-parent benefit and FIS; lower rate band of tax abolished.

April: Prescription charges raised to 70p and charges for dental treatment up; charge of £2 for a sight test (except for under-16s); season tickets to cost £12 pa or £4.50 for 4 months. Council house rents up on average by 21%. NI contributions up by 0.25%.

July: SSA 1980: provided for breaking of link between earnings and uprating and for changes to SB system. SS (No 2) Act 1980: provided for abolition of ERS, 5% abatement of short-term NI benefits and invalidity benefit and cuts in strikers' and various other benefits (see November 1980 and January 1982). Education (No 2) Act: LEAs ceased to be required to provide nursery education, school meals (other than for children in families in receipt of SB or FIS) and allowed LEAs to charge and provide what they wished.

November: SSA 1980: the SBC abolished and some functions replaced by the SSAC (see July 1980). The new SB scheme came into effect (see July 1980). NI and SB rates aligned, thus reducing supplementary pensions by 40p pw. Claimants lost 2 weeks of increase due to November uprating taking effect 2 weeks later than normally. Pensions and other long-term benefit increases linked to estimates of price rises only; consequently, lower than if still related to earnings. Short-term and invalidity benefits increased by 5% less than forecast of estimate of price rises (see July 1980). Changes made in method of uprating NI child dependency additions, resulting in cuts in real value of child support in this and subsequent years. FIS and mobility allowance raised by more than inflation.

December: Prescription charges up to £1. School-leavers denied SB until the end of the school holidays after they leave (see July 1980).

---

* Entries from May 1979 – April 1983 are a slightly edited version of that included in *Thatcherism and the poor*, appendix 1, by Ann Stanyer

1981

March: Budget: Personal tax allowances frozen but CB increased in line with inflation. SSA 1981: intention to clawback in November 1% overpaid in 1980 because of overestimate of inflation.

April: Social Security Contributions Act 1981: provided for increase in range of low earnings over which NI contributions paid and for a reduction in the Treasury supplement to the NI Fund, thus requiring an increase in contribution rates higher than that required by Government Actuary. Council house rents up on average by 45%. NI contributions up by 1%.

July. Extension of long-term rate of SB for men 60 or over if unemployed for 1 year or more and cease registering for work. Patrick Jenkin committed government to maintain CB at November 1980 value, subject to economic and other circumstances. The NIAC reported on housewives NCIP; DHSS statement on internal review still awaited at March 1983. Poverty figures to be published biennially rather than annually.

September: Education Act 1980: assisted places scheme came into effect; free school meals for assisted pupils in families in receipt of SB or FIS; half-price meals for assisted pupils not eligible for free meals but whose parents' income up to £4,000 pa. Initial uniform grants up to £80 and subsequent grants of £20-£40 every second year; free travel for pupils living more than 3 miles from school if parental income up to £4,600 and a sliding scale determining charges for those with higher incomes.

November: 1% clawback on benefit increases; shortfall in benefit uprating – 2% lower than inflation, except mobility allowance raised by more than rate of inflation.

December: Chancellor announced he would restore the shortfall only to certain long-term beneficiaries.

1982

January: SS(No 2) Act 1980: ERS to unemployment sickness, widows' and maternity benefits started to be phased out.

March: Budget: 2% shortfall to be restored for all benefits; CB to be increased in line with inflation; personal tax allowances to be raised by more than inflation; no statement on restoration of 5% abatement on UB when brought into tax (see July 1982); mobility allowance to be tax free. New mothers to receive CB monthly; existing recipients and a limited group of new recipients could opt to continue to receive a weekly payment (eg, single parents).

April: Prescription charges up to £1.30; glasses up from £8.30 to £15 per lens; charges for routine dental treatment from £9 max. to £13 max. Council house rents up on average by 19%. NI contributions up by 1%.

June: Government announced single mothers claiming one-parent benefit not to be asked about their sex lives. Self-certificatioin of sickness introduced.

July: UB becomes taxable; attempts by Conservative backbenchers to restore 5% abatement failed. Expectant mothers no longer required to satisfy NI contribution conditions to receive maternity grant (though have to satisfy 26-week residence rule).

September: Legal Aid Act 1982: legal aid extended to Mental Health Review Tribunals.

October: End of compulsory registration at job centres and consequent changes in method of counting unemployed and in availability for work test.

November: Social Security and Housing Benefits Act 1982: housing benefit payable to some council tenants in receipt of SB (see also April 1983). SB uprated on basis of RPI minus housing element, ie, at 0.5% less than other benefits. Increase in SB capital limit to £2,500. Chancellor announced intention to clawback this year's overestimate of rate of inflation.

December: Postal claims introduced for unemployed SB claimants.

1983

March: CB increased by 11% making good previous cut; tax allowances increased by 14%.

April: Industrial injury benefit abolished. SS & HB Act 1982: statutory sick pay introduced: first 8 weeks of sick pay responsibility of employers – low rates for low paid; no additions for dependants; taxable and subject to NI contributions. Prescription charges up to £1.40. NI contributions up by 0.25%. Housing benefit payable instead of rent rebates and allowances for all tenants and instead of rate rebates for tenants and owner-occupiers (see also November 1982).

April: Widespread chaos resulted from the implementation of HB. Thousands of tenants received either no benefit or the wrong amounts due to computer or administrative error. SHAC reported that 2.5m tenants are worse off as a result of the scheme. Regulations published allowing married women to claim NI dependency additions.

July: Prime minister refused to give assurance that unemployment benefit would be increased in line with inflation like other NI benefits.

August: Department of Employment stepped up drive against alleged fraud with the establishment of Regional Benefit Investigation Teams (see chapter 11).

October: DHSS Low Income Tables showed the rising tide of poverty in Great Britain.

November: Chancellor's Autumn statement: housing programme cut by £465m in 1984/5, HB by £230m; 5% abatement (see chapter 12) of UB, but not other benefits, made good; SSP does not compensate for 5% abatement of sickness benefit; benefits uprated on historical method, not prediction of inflation; increase 2% less than under old method. Invalidity trap abolished. Review of pensions announced.

December: Abolition of 'normal household duties test' and replacement of NCIP and HNCIP by severe disablement allowance announced.

1984

January: Conservative backbench revolt forced government to modify proposed HB benefit cut to £185m; SSAC reported that HB cuts were 'misconceived' and would 'cause substantial losses . . . to families who have very low incomes'. Tory MP Matthew Parris showed in a 'World in Action' programme the inability to survive a week on SB: 'It bloody well isn't easy on the dole.'

February: DHSS ordered major drive in 59 areas into alleged social security abuse:

UROs questioned 18- to 25-year-olds about why they left jobs; Society Security Policy Inspectorate interviewed young people not joining a YTS scheme. White Paper outlined huge reduction in spending on school meals from £414m in 1983/4 to £257m in 1984/5; Hertfordshire County Council first local authority to abolish school meals for all children except those statutorily entitled to them. Review of HB announced. Government refused to lend Britain's support to UN-sponsored International Year for the Homeless.

March: Further increase in prescription charges to £1.60. Budget: tax allowances raised by 12%. CB increases no longer announced as part of budget.

April: Secretary of state for social services announced 'the most comprehensive review of the social security system for 40 years.' Estimates showed 2.5m people worse off following HB cuts.

May: Review of maternity benefits announced.

June: November benefit upratings announced, together with cuts of over £100m; social security minister Rhodes Boyson said almost 2m disabled and elderly people faced benefit cuts of 50p to £1. CB increased by less than increase in personal tax allowances.

July: NSPCC reported 50% rise in the number of children injured by their parents between 1979 and 1982 and that one of main causes was unemployment-induced stress.

September: DHSS announced 6-month freeze on amounts of SB paid to people in board and lodgings and in private or voluntary residential homes.

October: Patrick Jenkin announced departmental enquiry into local government finance, including 'whether local democratic accountability could be improved by reducing rate rebates so that poor people would feel the full cost of council spending'. Most married women excluded from Community Programme by new regulation requiring CP people or their spouse to be on UB or SB.

November: Chancellor's Autumn statement: substantial restrictions on payment of SB for those in lodgings and private residential and nursing homes; proposed increase in the HB

153

children's needs allowance cancelled; 5% abatement in invalidity pension restored but invalidity pensioners no longer to receive both earnings related component and related invalidity allowance at the same time. Public expenditure on housing cut by £65m for 1985/6 although Treasury had planned £650m cut.

December: DHSS considered privatising 20 centres for single homeless people.

1985

— *January:* Social security commissioners ruled that strikers not entitled to FIS on basis of strike income.

— *February:* Social security minister announced that postal claiming to be made available to all SB claimants by end of May.

March: Budget: real increase in tax thresholds and restructuring of NI contributions announced; new regulations resulted in HB cuts of up to £5.47 pw for 110,000 tenants in high rent areas. DHSS announced regulations forcing unemployed 16-25-year-olds in board and lodgings to move every 2, 4 or 8 weeks according to area, or face big cuts in benefit.

April: 25% increase in dental charges, dentists claim that patients not exempt from charges would pay most of the cost of their treatment for the first time. Total abolition of 'half-test' rule announced.

May: Government Green Paper proposed means-testing home improvement grants. Her Majesty's Inspectorate of Schools reported expenditure cuts on school buildings adversely affecting the quality of education.

— *June:* Green Paper on the review of social security published (see chapter 12). 35p cut in CB announced as part of benefit uprating; 850,000 families with a young unemployed, disabled or pensioner relative living at home to have reduction in HB.

July: Following an earlier consultation paper, employment secretary announced intention to introduce early legislation to remove all young people under 21 from Wages Councils regulations and confine Councils to setting only a single minimum rate and a single overtime rate for those 21 and over. Proposals to allow employers to opt out of SSP published in consultative

document 'Lifting the burden'. MSC extended YTS to 2 years for 500,000 young people. Enquiry into British housing, chaired by Duke of Edinburgh, recommended abolition of mortgage interest tax relief.

August: High court found government restrictions on board and lodgings payments unlawful.

September: DHSS appealed against high court decision on board and lodgings regulations – government again defeated in court of appeal.

October: New temporary regulations to curb board and lodging SB payments also declared unlawful by House of Commons Statutory Instruments Committee; regulations subsequently withdrawn.

November: Environment secretary Kenneth Baker announced £185m cut in capital spending on housing; GLC reported 700% rise in official homelessness since 1970.

December: White Paper on Social Security published incorporating certain changes to the Green Paper, including proposal that SERPS not be abolished but modified.

1986

— *January:* Social Security Bill introduced into Commons. Secretary of state for Scotland announced replacement of domestic rates with poll tax on all adult residents.

February: Housing minister stated that rent controls for new tenants to be phased out after next general election. Cuts in legal aid, particularly hurting low income families with children, announced.

March: Budget: basic rate of income tax reduced to 29% and personal allowances raised by 5.7% in line with inflation; Low Pay Unit says will have no effect on poverty trap which has increased fivefold from 90,000 to 480,000 in past six years. Green Paper on Reform of Personal Taxation proposed transferable allowances for married couples.

April: European Court found Britain in breach of EEC law on sex discrimination by refusing to pay ICA to married and cohabiting women. SSP extended from 8 to 28 weeks.

May: White Paper 'Building businesses . . .

not barriers' proposed removing or reducing a number of employees' rights.

June: Comprehensive review of student grants, including possibility of introducing loans, announced. Government announced savings of £100m from cuts in HB.

July: Social Security Act 1986 and Wages Act 1986 receive Royal Assent. DHSS Low Income Family Tables released as House of Commons began summer recess. Restart scheme for long-term unemployed launched, including compulsory interviews to be offered a menu of options; if fail to attend or are deemed to have refused 'available work', risk having benefit suspended for up to 13 weeks (from October). Buckinghamshire county council became first local authority to vote to abolish school meals in primary and secondary schools.

August: cuts in SB single payments introduced (see chapter 12). Revised exceptionally severe weather payments scheme announced for some SB claimants. Department of Employment figures showed annual number of families accepted as homeless was 94,000.

October: under 1986 Social Security Act changes in the industrial injuries scheme implemented; voluntary unemployment penalty extended from 6 to 13 weeks and reduced rates of short-term NI benefits abolished. Announcement that benefits to be increased by 2% in April 1987. No restoration of the 35p cut in CB made in 1985. Expenditure on HB to be reduced by £68m; average loss of 47p per week for pensioners and 56p for other claimants. Tightening up of procedures for assessing availability for work of newly unemployed announced.

November: Chancellor's autumn statement: SSP to be cut by £18.5m pa, housing programme to be increased by 14%, for repairs to existing properties rather than new building.

1987

January: Government announced trigger temperature for exceptionally severe weather payments to be increased in response to 'severest weather for 40 years'. SB claimants under pension age to receive only half mortgage interest for first 4 months on benefit; further freeze on board and lodging SB payments announced.

March: Further increase in prescription charges announced; a 12-fold cash increase of 1,100% since 1979. Budget: basic rate of tax cut by 2p; personal allowances increased in line with inflation; Chancellor widely criticised for failing to help the unemployed and low paid. Health Education Council's Report, *The Health Divide,* published showing that social inequalities in health are widening in the 1980s.

April: abolition of £25 maternity grant for all mothers; women on FIS and SB can apply to the newly established social fund (see chapter 13); statutory maternity pay paid by employers replaces maternity benefit; abolition of death grant and replacement by help from social fund for those on FIS, SB or HB.

155

References

All *Hansard* references are to House of Commons debates. For abbreviations used, see notes at front.

CHAPTER 1: *Introduction: A policy for two nations* (pp 1-7)

1 D. Bull and P. Wilding (eds), *Thatcherism and the poor*, CPAG, 1983.
2 CPAG, *Poverty and the Labour government*, 1970; F. Field, *Children worse off under Labour?*, CPAG, 1978; F. Field, *Priority for children: a Labour success*, CPAG, 1978.
3 See also *The rising tide of poverty*, Low Pay Unit/CPAG, 1986.
4 As note 3, p 2.
5 Malcolm Dean, *Guardian*, 30 January 1980; David Donison, *The politics of poverty*, Martin Robertson, 1982, p 167; both quoted in Bull and Wilding, note 1 above, p 6.
6 N. Wapshott and G. Brock, *Thatcher*, Macdonald & Co, 1983.
7 F.A. Hayek, *Law, legislation and liberty*, vol 2, Routledge & Kegan Paul, 1976, p 87.
8 DHSS, *Reform of social security*, Cmnd 9517, HMSO, 1985, p 12.
9 *Hansard*, 6 April 1987, cols 42-3.
10 *Low Pay Review 29*, April 1987.
11 Wapshott and Brock, note 6 above.
12 *Guardian*, 5 March 1987.
13 See *The Times* (editorial) and *Guardian*, 16 April 1987.
14 P. Golding, 'Rethinking common sense about social policy', in Bull and Wilding, note 1 above, p 7.
15 See A. Walker, *Social planning*, Blackwell, 1984, ch 2.
16 *Observer*, 26 October 1986.
17 A. Walker, P. Ormerod and L. Whitty, *Abandoning social priorities*, CPAG, 1979.

CHAPTER 2: *The war on the poor* (pp 8-19)

1 P. Golding, 'Rethinking commonsense about social policy' in D. Bull and P. Wilding (eds), *Thatcherism and the poor*, CPAG, 1983.
2 See also, A. Walker, S. Winyard and C. Pond, 'Conservative economic policy:

the social consequences', as note 1.
3 As note 1, pp 9-10.
4 G. Gilder, *Wealth and poverty*, Buchan and Enright, 1982.
5 As note 4, p. 27.
6 K. Joseph and J. Sumption, *Equality*, Murray 1979, pp 27-8.
7 P. Ashton, Letters, *New Society*, 5 December 1986.
8 D. Marsland, 'Wages councils destroy jobs', *Economic Affairs*, January 1984.
9 As note 2
10 J. Bradshaw and J. Morgan, 'Budgeting on benefit', *New Society*, 6 March 1987.
11 B. Jordan and J. Greenwood, 'The dole quizz', *New Society* 16 January 1987.
12 R. Franey, *Poor Law*, CHAR/CPAG, 1983.
13 S. Weir, 'Housing nightmare', *New Society*, 27 January 1984.
14 Report in *Roof*, March/April 1985.
15 P. Johnson, 'Families under fire', *Daily Telegraph*, 5 January 1987.
16 C. Lasch, 'Making America feel good about itself', *New Statesman*, 29 August 1986.
17 N. Baldari, 'An estate of crisis', *New Society*, 27 February 1987.

CHAPTER 3: *The growth of poverty* (pp 20-26)
Sources of data
Central Statistical Office (CSO), *Economic Trends*, Annual Supplement, HMSO, 1987.
CSO, 'Incidence of taxes and benefits in 1979', *Economic Trends*, HMSO, January 1981.
CSO, 'Incidence of taxes and benefits in 1985', *Economic Trends*, HMSO, November 1986.
Cmnd 56-II, *The government's expenditure plans 1987-88 to 1989-90*, Volume II, HMSO, London, 1987.
Cmnd 9143-II, *The government's expenditure plans 1984-85 to 1986-87*, Volume II, HMSO, London, 1984.

Department of Employment, *Employment Gazette*, HMSO, February 1987.
Department of the Environment, *Homeless returns*, London, 1985 and earlier years.
Department of Health and Social Security (DHSS), *Social security statistics 1986*, HMSO, London, 1986.
DHSS, *Low income families 1983*, London, 1986.
Goldman Sachs, *The UK economics analyst*, London, February 1987.

Chapter 4: *Rich and poor: the growing divide* (pp 27-38)
1 DHSS, *Low income families 1979-83*, estimate for 1986 by House of Commons Library, in F. Field, *Freedom and wealth in a socialist future*, Constable, 1987.
2 *Independent*, 5 January 1987.
3 Quoted in R. Hemming, *Poverty and incentives*, Oxford University Press, 1984.
4 *Low Pay Review*, No 27, Autumn 1986.
5 W.W. Daniel, 'Who didn't get a pay increase last year?', *Policy Studies*, vol 5, pt 1, July 1984.
6 *Financial Times*, 11 March 1987.
7 *Low Pay Review 26*, Summer 1986.
8 For details of the effect of the Wages Act see *Low Pay Review 27* and *28*, and also *The Wages Act explained: a Low Pay Unit guide*, 1986.
9 See report in *Financial Times*, 18 July 1985.
10 House of Commons Employment Select Committee, oral evidence, 3 December 1986.
11 *Financial Times*, 19 January 1987, from HM Treasury, based on the *New Earnings Survey*.
12 *Hansard*, 17 July 1986, cols 606-8, based on single person.
13 Charterhouse, *Top Management Remuneration, UK, 1986/7*.
14 *A pittance from the government: the facts about low pay in the Civil Service*, Low Pay Unit/Civil Service Union, 1987.
15 *Hansard*, 10 February 1987, col 182; 13 January 1987, cols 150-2; 23 April 1986, col 176.
16 *Daily Telegraph*, 21 March 1986.
17 *Hansard*, 23 March 1987, col 34.
18 *Hansard*, 9 April 1986, cols 124-5.
19 House of Commons Library Research Note No 295; *Hansard*, 27 March 1986, cols 607-10; plus Low Pay Unit calculations.
20 Low Pay Unit, *The 1987 budget: a poor deal*, 1987, using figures derived from K.F. Wallis et al (eds), *Models of the UK economy: a third review by the ESRC Macro-Economic Modelling Bureau*, Oxford University Press, updated for 1987/88 in line with money GDP growth rate, table 2.1, *Financial statement and budget report*.
21 *The survey of personal incomes 1983-84*, Board of Inland Revenue, 1987.
22 *Low Pay Review 18*, Summer 1984.
23 *Hansard*, 9 April 1986, cols 125-6.
24 *Hansard*, 27 March 1986, col 606.
25 House of Commons Library, mimeo, published in F. Field, note 1 above.
26 CSO, *Social trends*, 1987; *Economic trends*, November 1986.
27 *Speech at St Lawrence Jewry*, 6 November 1985.
28 Own calculations from *Hansard*, 6 March 1987, cols 713-16; 2 March 1987, col 244; 7 November 1986, col 628.
29 The Sopcial Security Consortium, *Of little benefit*, 1986.
30 *Observer*, 25 May 1986.

Chapter 5: *Divided Britain* (pp 39-49).
1 Report of the Archbishop of Canterbury's Commission on urban priority areas, *Faith in the city*, Church House, 1986.
2 CSO, *Regional trends*, 1986.
3 Department of Employment (DOE), *Employment Gazette*, March 1987.
4 Bob Deacon, *Poverty and deprivation in the South-west*, CPAG 1987.
5 Steve Winyard, *Poverty and deprivation in Yorkshire and Humberside*, CPAG, 1987.
6 DOE, *New earnings survey*, 1979 and 1986.
7 As note 5.
8 DOE, *Family expenditure survey*, 1980 and 1985.
9 As note 7.

Chapter 6: *Impoverishing women* (pp 50-60).
1 S. Peace, 'The forgotten female: social policy and older women' in C. Phillipson and A. Walker (eds), *Ageing and social policy*, Gower, 1986.

2 A. Walker, 'The poor relation: poverty among older women' in C. Glendinning and J. Millar (eds), *Women and poverty in Britain*, Wheatsheaf Books, 1987.

3 J. Millar, 'Lone mothers', in Glendinning and Millar, see note 2.

4 L. Jordan and B. Waine, 'Women's income in and out of employment', *Critical Social Policy*, vol 6, no 3, 1986/7, pp 63-78.

5 Equal Opportunities Commission (EOC), *Annual report 1986*, OEC, 1987.

6 EOC, *Women and men in Britain: a statistical profile*, EOC, 1986.

7 Unemployment Unit, *Bulletin*, no 15, January 1985.

8 Jordan and Waine, see note 4.

9 S. Lonsdale, 'Patterns of paid work', in Glendinning and Millar, see note 2.

10 Department of Employment, *Employment Gazette*, vol 92, no 12, 1984, p 559.

11 O. Robinson and J. Wallace, 'Growth and utilization of part-time labour in Great Britain', *Employment Gazette*, September, 1984.

12 EOC, *Building businesses . . . not barriers: implications for women of the White Paper proposals relating to part-time workers and maternity rights*, Briefing Paper, EOC, 1986.

13 Lonsdale, see note 7.

14 A. McGoldrick, *Equal treatment in occupational pension schemes*, EOC, 1984.

15 J.C. Brown and S. Small, *Occupational benefits as social security*, PSI, 1985.

16 J.C. Brown and S. Small, *Maternity benefits: family income support part 9*, PSI, 1985.

17 S. Baloo, I. McMaster and K. Sutton, *Statutory sick pay: the failure of privatisation in social security*, Disability Alliance and Leicester, Rights Centre and City Council, 1986.

18 As note 19, p 55.

19 Welsh Women's Aid, *Available for work?*, 1982.

20 Claire Callender, 'Redundancy, unemployment and poverty', in Glendinning and Millar, see note 2.

21 Baloo et al, see note 19.

22 CPAG, *Welfare Rights Bulletin*, June, 1985.

23 A. Walsh and R. Lister, *Mother's Lifeline*, CPAG, 1985.

24 Social Security Consortium, *Of little benefit*, 1986, p 9.

25 As note 26, p 21.

26 Disability Alliance, *Social security White Paper: summary and comments*, 1985.

27 H. Land and S. Ward, *Women won't benefit*, NCCL, 1986, p 41.

28 Ruth Lister and Fran Bennett, *Opportunity lost*, CPAG, 1986.

29 *Daily Telegraph*, 5 June 1986.

30 *Hansard*, 15 July 1986.

31 Clare Ungerson (ed), *Women and social policy*, Macmillan, 1985, pp 213-14.

32 *Growing older: White Paper on services for elderly people*, Cmnd. 8173, HMSO, 1981, para 1.9.

33 C. Glendinning and P. Dixon, 'School meals: privatisatioin, stigma and local autonomy', in D. Bull and P. Wilding (eds), *Thatcherism and the poor*, CPAG, 1983.

34 H. Graham, 'Women's poverty and caring', in Glendinning and Millar, see note 4, p 238.

Chapter 7: *Second-class citizens* (pp 61-69)
1 This section draws upon the *1985 Labour Force Survey*, HMSO, 1986; and Anne Newnham, *Employment, unemployment and black people*, Runnymede Trust, 1986.

2 Colin Brown, *Black and white Britain*, PSI, 1984.

3 A. Newnham, see note 1.

4 *Guardian*, 6 April 1984.

5 *New Society*, 16 May 1986.

6 M. Cross and D. Smith (eds), *Black youth futures: ethnic minorities and the Youth Training Scheme*, National Youth Bureau, 1987.

7 D. Byrne (ed), *Waiting for change? working in hotel and catering*, Low Pay Unit, 1986.

8 C. Brown, see note 2.

9 C. Brown and P. Gay, *Racial discrimination: 17 years after the Act*, PSI, 1985.

10 *The Times*, 18 February 1987.

11 *A different reality: an account of black people's experiences and their grievances before and after the Handsworth rebellion of September 1985*, West Midlands County Council, 1986.

12 'From resistance to rebellion' in *A different hunger: writings on black resistance*, Pluto Press, 1982.
13 *Public Record Office*, file HO213/7 14.
14 This section has drawn on P. Gordon and A. Newnham, *Passport to benefits? racism in social security*, CPAG/Runnymede Trust, 1985.
15 See Steven Cooper, *Observations in supplementary benefits offices: reform of SB working paper C*, PSI, 1985.
16 Maryrose Tarpey, *English speakers only: a report of work on take-up . . .* , Islington Peoples Rights, 1984.
17 *Searchlight*, March 1985.
18 *The Broadwater Farm Inquiry: report of the independent inequiry into disturbances of October 1985* (chaired by Lord Gifford, QC), 1986.

Chapter 8: *Living with unemployment* (pp 70-81)

1 Nigel Lawson, budget statement, *Hansard*, 17 March 1987, col 815.
2 Second special report from the Treasury and Civil Service committee session 1982-93, *International monetary arrangements*, HMSO, May 1983, p xx.
3 M. White, *Long-term unemployment and labour markets*, PSI, December 1983, p 204, table III.7.
4 As note 3, p 39.
5 S. Moylan, J. Millar and R. Davies, *For richer or poorer? DHSS cohort study of unemployed men*, HMSO, 1984, p iv.
6 R. Berthoud, *Selective social security*, PSI, 1986, p 2.
7 J. Burgoyne, 'Unemployment and married life', *Unemployment Unit Bulletin*, no 18, November 1985.
8 M. Bartley, 'Unemployment, nutrition and health', *Unemployment Unit Bulletin*, no 17, July 1985.
9 K.A. Moser, A.J. Fox, D.R. Jones, 'Unemployment and mortality in the OPCS longitudinal study', *Lancet*, 8 December, pp 1324-29.
10 A. Scott-Samuel, *Lancet*, 22 December, pp 1464-5.
11 Rt Hon Kenneth Clarke MP addressing the MIND conference, 'Life after mental illness? Opportunities in an age of unemployment', Kensington Town Hall, 22-23 October 1984.
12 S. Platt and N. Kreitman, 'Parasuicide and unemployment among men in Edinburgh, 1968-82', *Psychological Medicine*, No 15, 1985, pp 113-23.
13 R. Smith, 'Occupationless health', *British Medical Journal*, 16 November 1985, p 1409.
14 This section draws heavily on: A. Sinfield and N. Fraser, *The real cost of unemployment*, Department of Social Administration, University of Edinburgh, March 1985, and D. Whitfield, *The annual cost of unemployment in Manchester*, Manchester Employment Plan, Manchester City Council, 1987.
15 H.M. Treasury, *The government's expenditure plans 1987-88 to 1989-90*, vol II, table 3.15.7.
16 As note 14, table 3.15.20.
17 *Hansard*, 25 July 1986, col 670.
18 See note 13.
19 *The jobs gap: measuring hidden unemployment*, Unemployment Unit Briefing No 10, Unemployment Unit, March 1986.
20 A. Rajin and R. Pearson (eds), *UK occupation and employment trends to 1990*, Butterworths, 1986.

Chapter 9: *Poor health* (pp 82-87)

1 The Black report, *Inequalities in Health*, London, DHSS, 1980.
2 See, for example, A. Gray, *On the Black Report: inequalities in health, a summary and a comment*, Health Economics Research Unit, University of Aberdeen, 1981; P. Townsend and N. Davidson (eds), *Inequalities in health: the Black Report*, Penguin Books, 1982; and Trades Union Congress, *The unequal health of the Nation, a TUC summary of the Black Report*, TUC, 1981.
3 M. Whitehead, *The health divide: inequalities in health in the 1980s*, Health Education Council, 1987.
4 As note 3.
5 M.G. Marmot, M.J. Shipley, and G. Rose, 'Inequalities in death: specific explanations of a general pattern?', *Lancet*, no i, 1984, pp 1003-6.
6 P. Townsend, P. Phillimore, and A. Beattie, *Inequalities in health in the Northern region*, The Northern Regional

159

Health Authority and the University of Bristol, 1986.

Chapter 10: *What happened to spending on the welfare state?* (pp88-100)
1 *The government's expenditure plans 1980-81*, HMSO, November 1979.
2 H of C Library, note 347, 11/1986.
3 *Hansard*, 6 April 1987, col 107.
4 This section draws heavily on A.B. Atkinson, J. Hills and J. Le Grand, *The welfare state in Britain 1970-1985: extent and effectiveness*, London School of Economics Welfare State Programme, Discussion Paper No 9, July 1986.
5 As note 2, in particular figure 1.
6 Figures 1 and 2 are based on data from the *United Kingdom National Accounts 1986*, Central Statistical Office. Figure 2 shows the stock of assets at the end of each calendar year.
7 See M. Ashworth, J. Hills and N. Morris, *Public finances in perspective*, Institute for Fiscal Studies Report Series No 8, 1984, table 1.8.
8 Figures for the value of tax reliefs from *The government's expenditure plans 1979-80 to 1982-83*, HMSO, 1900, table 16, and *The government's expenditure plans 1987-88 to 1989-90*, HMSO, 1984, table 2.29.

Chapter 11: *Reforming social security: despite the claimant* (pp 101-109)
1 Figures provided by the House of Commons library.
2 *Hansard*, 10 December 1979, col 897.
3 *Reform of social security* (Green Paper), Cmnd 9517, HMSO, June 1985.
4 See note 3, p 2.
5 *Hansard*, 26 March 1980, col 1463.
6 *The Conservative manifesto*, Conservative Central Office, 1983, p 26.
7 Roger Smith, 'Who's fiddling? fraud and abuse', in S. Ward (ed), *DHSS in crisis*, CPAG, 1985.
8 See, for example, S. Coetzee, *Flat broke: has the welfare state collapsed in Birmingham*, Birmingham Welfare Rights Group, 1983.
9 See note 7.
10 *Hansard*, 27 March 1980, col 1660.
11 See note 3 above, p 3.
12 See note 7.
13 9,000 people were convicted of social security offences in 1983, compared with 136 for tax offences, *Guardian*, 25 March 1987.
14 See Ros Franey, *Poor Law*, CHAR/CPAG, 1983.
15 C. Walker, *The reform of the supplementary benefits scheme*, University of Leeds, 1984, p 59.
16 See note 3, para 4.4.
17 R. Berthoud, *The reform of supplementary benefit*, PSI, 1984.
18 See note 15.
19 I. Cole-Hamilton and T. Lang, *Tightening belts*, London Food Commission, 1986.
20 L. Burghes, *Living from hand to mouth*, FUS/CPAG, 1980.
21 See note 19.
22 See, for example, K. Cooke and Sally Baldwin, *How much is enough?*, Family Policy Studies Centre, 1984.
23 DHSS, *Reform of the SB Scheme* (White Paper), Cmnd 7773, November 1979, para 4.5.
24 SSAC, *Fifth report of the Social Security Advisory Committee 1986/7*, London, HMSO, 1987, p 23.
25 See note 3, p 18.
26 S. Baloo et al, *Statutory sick pay: the failure of privatisation in Social Security*, Leicester City Council/DAERA, 1986.
27 See note 24, para 8.8.

Chapter 12: *The bottom line* (pp 110-115)
1 The benefit rates used in this chapter are those current from April 1987.
2 *Hansard*, 24 July 1976, cols 408-9.
3 DHSS, *Social assistance*, 1978.
4 *Fifth report of the Social Security Advisory Committee 1986/7*, para 1.61.
5 Quoted in Social Security Advisory Committee, *First Report*, 1981.
6 H of C Library, note 347, 11/1986.
7 *The government expenditure plans 1986/7-1988/9*, HMSO, 1986.
8 *EEC directive on equal treatment*, 19 December 1978. The directive came into force on 20 December 1984.
9 HM Treasury, *The reform of personal taxation*, HMSO, 1986.
10 DHSS *Reform of social security: programme for change*, HMSO 1985.

Chapter 13: *What future for social security?* (pp 120-128)
1 Social Security Consortium, *Of little*

benefit, SSC, November 1986.
2 *Sunday Times*, 8 April 1984.
3 DHSS, *Reform of social security* (Green Paper), HMSO, 1985, Vol 2, paras 1.7 and 6.6; Vol 1, paras 6.3 and 1.12.
4 *Reform of social security: a checklist of the responses of 60 key organisations to the government's Green Paper*, compiled by Angela Hadjipateras, CPAG, November 1985.
5 See, for example, speech by Rt Hon Norman Fowler MP, secretary of state for social services, on 26 October 1985 to the Sutton Coldfield Conservative Association.
6 White Paper, *Reform of Social Security: programme for action*, Cmnd 9691, HMSO, 1985.
7 For a description of the progress of different aspects of the Bill through Parliament, see note 1.
8 Technical Annexe to White Paper, see note 6.
9 As note 1, p 15.
10 Social Services Select Committee, Seventh Repport, *The government's Green Paper, 'reform of social security'*, HMSO, 1985, paras 9 and 48.
11 Social Security Advisory Committee, *Fifth Report 1986/7*, HMSO, 1987, para 2.3.5.
12 See note 11, para 2.3.6.
13 As note 1, p 3.
14 DHSS, *Social Security Statistics 1983*, HMSO, 1983.
15 As note 10, para 13.
16 As note 6.
17 Rt Hon Francis Pym MP, *Hansard*, 28 January 1986, col 841.

Chapter 14: *Conclusion I: A divided Britain* (pp 129-138)
1 A Walker, 'Selective statistics', *Social Services Insight*, 30 August 1986.
2 *Hansard*, 5 May 1983, cols 139-40, and 10 March 1987, cols 101-2.
3 J. Bradshaw and J. Morgan, 'Budgeting on benefit', *New Society*, 6 March 1987.
4 HM Treasury, *Inland revenue statistics*, London, HMSO, 1986; see also M. Wicks, 'The decade of inequality', *New Society*, 6 February 1987.
5 A. Walker, S. Winyard and C. Pond, 'Conservative economic policy: the social consequences' in D. Bull and P. Wilding (eds), *Thatcherism and the poor*, CPAG, 1983.
6 *Guardian*, 27 March 1987.
7 *Guardian*, 28 March 1987.
8 *Observer*, 5 April 1987.
9 *Hansard*, 11 March 1985.
10 Speech at St Lawrence Jewry, 6 November 1985, p 2.
11 A.H. Halsey, 'Social trends since World War II', *Social Trends 17*, HMSO, 1987, p 17.
12 A. Gamble, 'The North South divide', *Marxism Today*, March 1987.
13 See note 10, p 7 (my italics).
14 *Low Pay Review 29*, Low Pay Unit, 1987.
15 Lord Chancellor's Department, *Legal aid in England and Wales: a new framework*, HMSO, 1987.
16 See, for example, *Daily Express*, 18 March 1987.
17 See CPAG, *Building one nation*, 1987.
18 *Financial Times*, 1 July 1986.
19 *UK regional development programme 1986-90*, papers released by Gordon Brown MP, 20 October 1986.
20 NEDC, *The British labour market and unemployment*, February 1987.
21 See L. Burghes, *Made in the USA: a review of workfare*, Unemployment Unit, 1987.
22 J. Mack and S. Lansley, *Poor Britain*, Allen & Unwin, 1984.

Chapter 15: *Conclusion II: There is an alternative* (pp 139-150)
1 *Daily Telegraph*, 25 March 1985.
2 John Lee in a Granada TV interview, February 1987, quoted in the *Guardian*, 24 March 1987.
3 *Daily Express*, 23 March 1987.
4 cf *Independent*, 12 February 1987.
5 For CPAG's critique of transferable allowances, see R. Lister and F. Bennett, *Opportunity lost*, CPAG, 1986.
6 See Charlie Leadbeater of the *Financial Times* writing in *Marxism Today*, April 1987.
7 M. Wicks, *A future for all*, Pelican, 1987, p 9.
8 Report of the Archbishop of Canterbury's Commission on Urban Priority Areas, *Faith in the city*, Church House, 1985, para 9.45.
9 Social Policy Committee of the Board for Social Responsibility, *Not just for the*

poor, Church House, 1986, para 7.37.
10 T.H. Marshall, *Sociology at the crossroads*, Heineman, republished 1963.
11 See R. Lister and F. Bennett, *Opportunity knocks*, CPAG, 1986.
12 For a discussion, see M. Desai, 'Drawing the Line: on defining the poverty threshold' in P. Golding (ed), *Excluding the poor*, CPAG, 1986.
13 *Day 1/Year 1: alternatives to the Social Security Act 1986*, Social Security Consortium, 1987.
14 For a detailed summary of these proposals, see the election pack produced by CPAG with the Low Pay Unit and Church Action on Poverty.
15 SDP/Liberal Alliance, *More jobs in a fairer Britain*, 1987.

16 .D. Owen and D. Steel, *The time has come*, Weidenfeld, 1987.
17 All quotations from NEC Statement on Social Security and Taxation to 1986 Labour Conference.
18 See D. Bull and P. Wilding (eds), *Thatcherism and the poor*, CPAG, 1983, ch 3.
19 See note 8, para 6.57.
20 *Observer*, 9 June 1985.
21 *Hansard*, 1 May 1986, cols 479-80.
22 *Hansard*, 29 January 1987, col 374.
23 *Hansard*, 15 April 1986, col 355.
24 *Daily Telegraph*, 17 October 1986.
25 N. Bosanquet, 'Public spending and the welfare state' in R. Jowell, S. Witherspoon, and L. Brook (eds), *British social attitudes, the 1986 report*, Gower, 1986, p 133.

Now's the time to join CPAG!

We can help you . . . with the facts on poverty.
You can help us . . . in the fight against poverty.

CPAG membership gives you access to all the latest – on welfare rights, income inequalities, perspectives on policy, and lots more!

And CPAG members give us the support we need to ensure that poverty is at the heart of the agenda, whatever political party is in power.

Send off the form now, and join CPAG in working for a fairer future.

Please complete and send to: CPAG, 4th Floor, 1-5 Bath Street, London EC1V 9PY.

I would like to join CPAG as a comprehensive member .... (tick)
(Comprehensive members receive CPAG's regular journal, Poverty, plus welfare rights and social policy publications – for £30/year).

or I would like information about other membership options .... (tick)

I enclose a cheque/PO (made out to CPAG) for £30 .... (tick)

Name _____

Organisation (if applicable) _____

Address _____

_____

_____ Postcode _____

162